550 Books on Buddhism

Bhagavan Tathāgata Śākyamuni Buddha

550 Books on Buddhism

Translations, Studies, and General Readings

550 BOOKS ON BUDDHISM

Translations, Studies, and General Readings
with Reference Works and 26 Related Texts

Edited by Elizabeth Cook and Ruth Fellhauer

Prepared and published by the Nyingma Institute,
1815 Highland Place, Berkeley, California 94709
in cooperation with Dharma Publishing,
2425 Hillside Place, Berkeley, California 94704 USA

ISBN 0-913546-97-6

Typeset in Fototronic Caledonia, printed, and
bound by Dharma Press, Oakland, California

9 8 7 6 5 4 3 2 1

Dedicated to all students of the Dharma

Contents

MAHĀYĀNA CANONICAL TEXTS

PĀLI TEXTS

BOOKS ON BUDDHISM

RELATED READINGS AND REFERENCE

Foreword

A wealth of the Buddhist teachings has been preserved for more than 2,500 years. Over the centuries, outstanding masters of the traditions have systematized and commented on the original teachings, and prepared manuals for study and practice of the Dharma. The life and teachings of the Buddha have inspired poetry, dramas, and epics that brought the meaning of the teachings alive for generations of human beings of all backgrounds and levels of spiritual development. In written and artistic forms, the Buddhist teachings have spread throughout Asia; enriched by masters of many Asian lands, they form a treasury of spiritual wisdom that we can draw upon today.

Although the work of translation is far from complete, Buddhist texts have been appearing in western languages for more than a hundred years. Recently, the growth of western interest in the Dharma has stimulated writings on Buddhism by westerners as well as traditional masters. Dharma students in the West now have access to a wide range of traditional texts and modern works to assist their efforts to study and practice the Buddhist teachings. Yet the availability of so much information can be confusing to beginners who lack a basic orientation to the teachings and an understanding of the nature and history of Dharma

Since 1973, when the Nyingma Institute was established, I have encouraged the faculty to prepare listings of recommended readings as guides for beginning students. Several years ago, the Dharma Publishing staff prepared comprehensive bibliographies of canonical texts for the Catalogue of the Nyingma Edition of the bKa'-'gyur and bsTan-'gyur. Recently I asked the faculty and staff of Nyingma Institute and Dharma Publishing to combine their efforts and compile a new listing of translations, introductory works, background readings, and basic reference works that would be helpful to beginners and advanced students alike. *Books on Buddhism* is the result of their cooperative research.

I hope that this bibliography will encourage anyone interested in the Dharma to read widely, deepening their knowledge of the Buddhist teachings and of the traditions which have preserved their vitality. A basic understanding of the vision and purpose of Dharma study is an invaluable support for practice, providing a foundation for overcoming all obstacles to realization.

Students who wish to broaden their research will find more detailed bibliographies of manuscripts, editions, and translations in the Catalogue of the Nyingma Edition. The Yeshe De Project, jointly sponsored by TNMC, Dharma Publishing, and the Nyingma Institute, is planning projects that will support intensive study and translation of Buddhist texts. If scholars and students concerned with the success of Dharma transmission are supportive of these activities, we may be able to develop cooperative exchanges of research information that will benefit Dharma students throughout the world.

Tarthang Tulku
December 1984

Guide to the Bibliography

This bibliography of suggested readings is organized by subject to help readers unfamiliar with the formal names of the original texts and their translation titles. Full bibliographic references are given under the title of original texts as they appear on the title page of the translation, with cross-references given under the full Sanskrit title.

For texts preserved in Pāli, the canonical works are listed in the order they appear in the Canon, with additional texts given in alphabetical order according to their English titles. In the remaining sections, books are alphabetized according to author or title; a few texts that are particularly important to several categories are listed in both.

This listing is not intended to be comprehensive, but rather to serve as a guide to basic works available in libraries and bookstores that have collections on Asian studies. Perhaps the subject organization will encourage the reader to brouse through each section and become acquainted with the names and titles of the basic texts and commentaries, together with modern publications and research materials on Buddhism.

A special section on general introductory works was prepared with the beginning reader in mind; all the books listed here are recommended as helpful starting points for those new to the Dharma teachings. Parents wishing to provide their children with books that encourage compassion and non-violence may be interested in the section on children's books, included in this listing for the first time. We hope that this small book will stimulate interest in studying the Dharma among readers of all ages, and that it will serve as a helpful guide to both beginning and advanced students.

As a special service to readers of this bibliography, Dharma Publishing Bookstore, located in the Nyingma Institute in Berkeley, can supply many of the books listed here. Entries which can be ordered directly from the Bookstore are coded DPB together with their current retail prices. Information on the bookstore and its services is provided at the end of the bibliography.

Mahāyāna
Canonical Texts

Vinaya and Sūtras

Adhyardhaśatakā-prajñāpāramitā-sūtra. *See* The Short Prajñāpāramitā Texts.

Amitāyur-dhyāna-sūtra. *See* Buddhist Mahāyāna Texts.

1. "Annotated Translation of the Daśabhūmika-sūtra," translated by Meguro Honda, revised by Johannes Rahder. *Studies in South, East, and Central Asia,* presented as a memorial volume to the late Prof. Raghu Vira by the members of the Permanent International Altaistic Conference. New Delhi: International Academy of Indian Culture, 1968. (Śatapiṭaka Series 74). Translation, pp. 115–276. An important Mahāyāna teaching on the ten stages of the Bodhisattva, traditionally included in the Avataṁsaka-sūtra.

Aṣṭasāhasrikā-prajñāpāramitā. *See* The Perfection of Wisdom in 8000 Lines.

Bhadracarī-praṇidhānarāja. *See* The Hymn of the Life and Vows of Samantabhadra.

2. *The Bhadramāyākāravyākaraṇa,* translated by Konstanty Régamey. Warsaw, 1938. (The Warsaw Society of Sciences and Letters. Publication of the Oriental Commission 3). Complete English translation.

Bhaiṣajyaguru-sūtra. *See* The Healing Buddha.

3. *Bhavasaṅkrānti-Sūtra and Nāgārjuna's Bhavasaṅkrānti-Śāstra with the Commentary of Maitreyanātha.* Translated by N. Aiyaswami Sastri. Madras: Adyar Library, 1938. Complete English translation, with Tibetan and restored Sanskrit texts.

4. *Buddhist Mahāyāna Texts,* edited by F. Max Müller. Oxford: Clarendon Press, 1894. (Sacred Books of the East 49). Paperback reprint, New York: Dover, 1969. Contains E. B. Cowell's translation of the Buddhacarita, chapters 1-17; Max Müller's translations of the larger and smaller Sukhāvatī-vyūha, the Vajracchedikā-prajñāpāramitā, and the Prajñāpāramitā-hṛdaya, as well as J. Takakusu's translation of the Amitāyur-dhyāna-sūtra. DPB $6.50

5. *Buddhist Monastic Discipline: The Sanskrit Prātimokṣa Sūtras of the Mahāsāṁghikas and Mūlasarvāstivādins,* edited by Charles S. Prebish. University Park: Pennsylvania State University Press, 1975. A primary Vinaya text containing guidelines for Buddhist monks. DPB $16.95

6. *Buddhist Texts From Japan,* edited by F. Max Müller. New York: AMS Press, 1976. Reprint of the 1881–1884 Oxford Edition. Contains the Diamond Sūtra (Vajracchedikā Prajñāpāramitā), a literal translation of Sanghavarman's Chinese version of four verses of the Sukhāvatīvyūha (chapters 4, 9, 31, 44), with portions of the Sanskrit text, together with the Heart Sūtra (Prajñāpāramitā Hṛdaya), with the Sanskrit text.

7. *Buddhist Thought and Asian Civilization.* Addresses, essays, and lectures in honor of Herbert V. Guenther, edited by S. Kawamura and Keith Scott. Berkeley: Dharma Publishing, 1977. Contains a complete translation by Akira Yuyama of the Svalpākṣarā Prajñāpāramitā Sūtra, and the Sanskrit and Tibetan texts. DPB $25.00

8. *Buddhist Wisdom Books: The Diamond and Heart Sūtras,* translated by Edward Conze. London: Allen & Unwin, 1975. Includes the Sanskrit text and the translator's commentary. DPB $7.50

9. *La Concentration de la marche héroique (Śūraṅgamasamādhisūtra),* translated by Étienne Lamotte. Bruxelles: Institut Belge des Hautes Études Chinoises, 1975. Complete French translation.

Daśabhūmika-sūtra. *See* Annotated Translation of the Daśabhūmika-sūtra.

10. *Dhammapada.* Tibetan text, English translation, vocabulary, glossary of basic technical Buddhist terms, and explanations of Tibetan grammar. Berkeley: Dharma Publishing. Forthcoming 1985. Prepared for the beginning student of Tibetan. For additional translations of this text *See* nos. 118–119.

Dharmapada. *See* The Gandhāri Dharmapada.

Diamond Sūtra. *See* Buddhist Texts from Japan; Buddhist Wisdom Books; Short Prajñāpāramitā Texts.

11. *The Diamond Sūtra: Three Mongolian Versions of the Vajracchedikā Prajñāpāramitā,* translated by Nicholas Poppe. Wiesbaden: Harrassowitz, 1971. (Asiatische Forschungen 35). Includes notes and glossaries.

12. *L'Enseignement de Vimalakīrti (Vimalakīrtinirdeśa),* translated by Étienne Lamotte. Louvain: Institut Orientaliste, Publications Universitaires, 1962. Complete French translation with detailed and informative notes. *See also* The Teaching of Vimalakīrti, an English translation of this work.

13. *The Flower Ornament Scripture,* translated from the Chinese by Thomas Cleary. 3 vols. Boulder: Prajñā Press, 1983– . Vol. I, books 1–25; vols. II and III forthcoming. A primary text of the Hua-yen school.
DPB (vol. I) $35.00

14. *Gaṇḍavyūha: Search for Enlightenment,* translated by Mark Ehman. Ph.D. dissertation. Ann Arbor: University Microfilms, 1977. Translations of chapters 1, 4, 5, 6, 18, 19. Traditionally part of the Avataṁsaka-sūtra; a third turning teaching.

15. *Gandhāri Dharmapada,* translated by J. Brough. London: Oxford University Press, 1962. From a unique manuscript.

16. *The Healing Buddha (Bhaiṣajyaguru),* translated by Raoul Birnbaum. Boulder: Shambhala, 1979. English translation of three texts from the Chinese Canon.
DPB $8.95

Heart Sūtra. *See* Buddhist Texts From Japan: Buddhist Wisdom Books; Short Prajñāpāramitā Texts.

17. *The Holy Teaching of Vimalakīrti: A Mahāyāna Scripture,* translated by Robert A. F. Thurman. University Park: Pennsylvania State University Press, 1976. Translated from the Tibetan with bibliographical references, notes, glossaries.
DPB $16.95

18. "The Hymn of the Life and Vows of Samantabhadra (Bhadracarī-praṇidhānarāja)," translated by Hokei Izumi. *Eastern Buddhist* 5 (1929–1931):226–247.

Samādhirāja-sūtra. *See* Three Chapters from the Samādhirājasūtra.

Lalitavistara-sūtra. *See* The Twelve Deeds of the Buddha; The Voice of the Buddha.

19. *The Laṅkāvatāra Sūtra: A Mahāyāna Text,* translated from the Sanskrit by D. T. Suzuki. Boulder: Prajñā Press, 1978. An important third turning teaching; a major source for doctrines developed in the Yogācāra school. DPB $15.00

20. *The Large Sutra on Perfect Wisdom, with the Divisions of the Abhisamayālaṅkāra,* translated by Edward Conze. Reprint ed. Berkeley: University of California, 1975. Abridged translation of the Pañcaviṁśatisāhasrikā, the Prajñāpāramitā teaching in 25,000 lines; some chapters are taken from the Aṣṭadaśasāhasrikā, the Prajñāpāramitā teaching in 18,000 Lines. DPB $40.00

21. *The Lion's Roar of Queen Śrīmālā: A Buddhist Scripture of the Tathāgatagarbha Theory,* translated by Alex and Hideko Wayman. New York: Columbia University Press, 1974. DPB $17.95

22. *Le Lotus de la Bonne Loi,* translated from the Sanskrit by Eugène Burnouf. Reprint ed. Paris: A. Maisonneuve, 1973. Complete French translation of the Saddharmapuṇḍarīka-sūtra. First published in 1852.

Mahāratnakūṭa-sūtra. *See* A Treaury of Mahāyāna Sūtras.

23. *The Mahāyānapārinirvāṇa-sūtra,* translated by Kosho Yamamoto. 3 vols. Ubeshi, Japan: Karinbunko, 1973–1975. (The Karin Buddhological Series 5). Complete English translation.

Pañcaśatikā-prajñāpāramitā-sūtra. *See* The Short Prajñāpāramitā Texts.

24. *The Perfection of Wisdom in 8000 Lines and its Verse Commentary,* translated from the Sanskrit by Edward Conze. 3rd printing. San Francisco: Four Seasons Foundation, 1983. A complete translation of the Ratnaguṇa-sañcāya-gāthā and the Aṣṭasāhasrikā-prajñāpāramitā-sūtra, basic Mahāyāna texts.
DPB $8.95

Prajñāpāramitā-hṛdaya. *See* Buddhist Mahāyāna Texts; Buddhist Texts From Japan; Buddhist Wisdom Books; Short Prajñāpāramitā Texts.

Prātimokṣa-sūtra. *See* Buddhist Monastic Discipline.

25. *The Question of Rāṣṭrapāla (Rāṣṭrapāla-paripṛcchā),* translated and annotated by Jacob Ensink. Zwolle: Van de Erven J. J. Tijl, 1952.

Rāṣṭrapāla-paripṛcchā. *See* The Question of Rāṣṭrapāla.

Ratnaguṇa-sañcāya-gāthā. *See* The Perfection of Wisdom in 8000 Lines.

Mahāratnakūṭa-sūtra. *See* A Treasury of Mahāyāna Sūtras.

26. *The Saddharmapuṇḍarīka, or The Lotus of the True Law,* translated by H. Kern. Reprint of 1884 ed. New York: Dover, 1963. DPB $6.00

Saddharmapuṇḍarīka sūtra. *See also* Le Lotus de la bonne loi; Scripture of the Lotus Blossom of the Fine Dharma.

27. *Saṁdhinirmocana Sūtra: L'Explication des mystères,* translated by Étienne Lamotte. Louvain: Bureau de Recueil; Paris: Adrien-Maisonneuve, 1935. Complete French translation of this important third turning teaching.

28. *Scripture of the Lotus Blossom of the Fine Dharma (Saddharmapuṇḍarīka),* translated from the Chinese of Kumārajīva by Leon Hurvitz. New York: Columbia University Press, 1976. Includes bibliographical references and index. A detailed scholarly translation. DPB $15.95

29. *The Short Prajñāpāramitā Texts,* translated by Edward Conze. American ed. Totowa, N. J.: Rowman & Littlefield, 1974. Contents: Suvikrāntavikrāmi, Adhyardhaśatikā, Vajracchedikā, Hṛdaya, Pañcaśatikā, and other Prajñāpāramitā-sūtras. DPB $20.00

Śrīmālādevī-siṁhanāda-sūtra. *See* The Lion's Roar of Queen Śrīmālā.

Sukhāvatīvyūha-sūtra, larger and smaller. *See* Buddhist Mahāyāna Texts.

Śūraṅgamasamādhisūtra. *See* La Concentration de la marche héroique.

30. *The Śūraṅgama Sūtra (Len yen ching),* translated from the Chinese by Lu K'uan Yu (Charles Luk). London: Rider, 1966. Complete English translation.

31. *The Śūraṅgama Sūtra,* translated from the Chinese by the Buddhist Text Translation Society, with commentary by Tripitaka Master Hsuan Hua. 6 vols. San Francisco: 1977–1981.

32. *The Sūtra of Golden Light,* translated by R. E. Emmerick. Reprint ed. London: Luzac, 1979. Complete English translation of the Suvarṇaprabhāṣottama-sūtra.

Suvikrāntavikrāmi-prajñāpāramitā. *See* The Short Prajñāpāramitā Texts.

33. *Suvarṇaprabhāṣottama-Sūtra: Das Goldglanz-Sūtra, ein Sanskrittext des Mahāyāna Buddhismus,* translated by Johannes Nobel. Leiden: Brill, 1958. Complete German translation.

Suvarṇaprabhāṣottama-sūtra. *See also* The Sūtra of Golden Light.

Svalpakṣarā-prajñāpāramitā. *See* Buddhist Thought and Asian Civilization; Short Prajñāpāramitā Texts.

34. *The Teaching of Vimalakīrti (Vimalakīrtinirdeśa),* translated from the French of Étienne Lamotte by Sara Boin. London: Pali Text Society, 1976.

35. *Three Chapters from the Samādhirājasūtra,* translated by Konstanty Régamey. Warsaw, 1938. (Publication of the Oriental Commission 3). English translation of chapters 8, 19, and 22, with Sanskrit and Tibetan texts.

36. *The Threefold Lotus Sutra (Saddharmapuṇḍarīka),* translated by Bunno Kato, Yoshiro Tamura, and Kojiro Miyasaka, with revisions by W. E. Soothill, Wilhelm Schiffler, and Pier P. Del Campana. New York: Weatherhill, 1975 DPB $10.95

37. *A Treasury of Mahāyāna Sūtras: Selections from the Mahāratnakūṭa Sūtra,* translated from the Chinese by the Buddhist Association of the United States. Garma C. C. Chang, general editor. Univer-

sity Park: Pennsylvania State University Press, 1983. Contains 22 of the 49 sūtras of the Mahāratnakūṭa, an important third turning teaching, with notes and glossaries. DPB $22.50

38. *The Twelve Deeds of the Buddha (Lalitavistara)*, translated from the Mongolian by Nicholas Poppe. Wiesbaden: Harrassowitz, 1967. (Asiatische Forschungen 23) Translation of chapters 6–9 of an abridged Tibetan version of the sūtra prepared by Cho-kyi 'od-zer.

39. *Udānavarga: A Collection of Verses from the Buddhist Canon, being the Northern Buddhist Version of the Dhammapada*, translated from the Tibetan of the bKa'-'gyur by William W. Rockhill. Reprint ed. Amsterdam: Oriental Press, 1975.

40. *Ugraparipṛcchā, the Mahāratnakūṭasūtra, and Early Mahāyāna Buddhism*, translated by Nancy Joann Schuster. Ph.D. dissertation, University of Toronto, 1976. Complete English translation, forthcoming in published edition, entitled *The Question of Ugra.*

41. *Vajracchedikā Prajñāpāramitā*, edited and translated with introduction and glossary by Edward Conze. 2nd ed. with corrections and additions. Rome: IsMEO, 1974. (Serie Orientale Roma 13). Sanskrit edition with complete English translation.

Vajracchedikā Prajñāpāramitā. *See also* Buddhist Mahāyāna Texts; Buddhist Texts from Japan; Buddhist Wisdom Books; Diamond Sūtra; Short Prajñāpāramitā Texts.

Vimalakīrtinirdeśa. *See* L'Enseignement de Vimalakīrti; The Holy Teaching of Vimalakīrti; The Teaching of Vimalakīrti.

42. *The Voice of the Buddha: The Beauty of Compassion (Lalitavistara-sūtra).* 2 vols. Berkeley: Dharma Publishing, 1983. The life of the Buddha expressed in verse and poetic prose; a fine edition, with 34 full-color plates of Tibetan thankas and glossary. Highly recommended for beginning and advanced students. DPB $55.00/boxed set

Abhidharma

Abhidharmahṛdaya. *See below:* The Essence of Metaphysics.

43. *Abhidharmakoça de Vasubandhu,* translated by L. de la Vallée Poussin. Paris: Paul Geuthner; Louvain: J.-B. Istas, 1923–1931. (Mélanges Chinoises et Bouddhiques 16). Reprinted 1971. Complete French translation of this essential Abhidharma text. Includes root verses and autocommentary.

44. *Le Compendium de la super-doctrine (Philosophie), (Abhidharmasamuccaya) d'Asaṅga,* translated by Walpola Rahula. Paris: École Française d'Extrême-Orient, 1971. Reprinted 1980. A complete French translation of the foundation text of the 'Higher Abhidharma'.

45. *The Essence of Metaphysics: Abhidharmahṛdaya,* translated and annotated by Charles Willemen. Bruxelles: Publications de l'Institut Belge des Hautes Études Bouddhiques, 1975.

Prajñāpāramitā

46. *Abhisamayālaṅkāra,* translated by Edward Conze. Translated from the original text with Sanskrit/Tibetan index. Rome: IsMEO, 1954. (Serie Orientale Roma 6). Complete English translation, with extensive glossary and index. Reprint in preparation.

Mādhyamika

47. *Akṣara-śatakam (The Hundred Letters), A Madhyamaka Text by Āryadeva.* Translated by Vasudev V. Gokhale. Heidelburg: Institut für Buddhismus, 1930. (Materialien zur Kunde des Buddhismus, Heft 14).

Āryadeva. Akṣaraśataka. *See* Akṣaraśataka.

Atīśa (Dīpaṁkāraśrījñāna). Bodhipathā-pradīpa. *See* A Lamp for the Path.

Bhavaviveka. Madhyamārthasaṅgraha. *See* Madhyamārthasaṅgraha of Bhavaviveka.

48. *Bodhicaryāvatāra. Introduction à la pratique des futurs Bouddhas, poème de Çāntideva.* Translated by L. de la Vallée Poussin. Paris: Librairie Bloud et çie, 1907. xii, 144 pp. Complete French translation.

Candrakīrti. Prasannapadā. *See* Candrakīrti's Clear Words; Lucid Exposition of the Middle Way.

49. *Candrakīrti's Clear Words, a Commentary on Nāgārjuna's Treatise on the Middle Way,* translated by Jeffrey Hopkins. Dharamsala: Library of Tibetan Works and Archives, 1976. English translation of chapter 2 of the Prasannapadā.

50. *Candragomin and the Bodhisattva Vow*, translated by Mark Tatz. Ph.D. dissertation, University of British Columbia, 1978. Complete English translation of the Bodhisattvasaṁvaraviṁśaka.

51. *The Conception of Buddhist Nirvana*, by Th. Stcherbatsky. Reprint ed. Delhi: Motilal Banarsidass, 1978. Contains the Sanskrit text of Nāgārjuna's Madhyamakakārikā with English translation of the chapters on causality and nirvana. DPB $12.95

52. *The Dialectical Method of Nāgārjuna: Vigrahavyāvartanī*, translated from the original Sanskrit by K. Bhattacharya; text critically edited by E. H. Johnston and Arnold Kunst. Delhi: Motilal Banarsidass, 1978. Complete translation. DPB $12.00

53. *Emptiness: A Study in Religious Meaning*, by Frederick Streng. New York: Abingdon Press, 1967. Includes complete English translations of the Mūlamadhyamaka-kārikā and Vigrahavyāvartanī.

54. *Entering the Path of Enlightenment (Bodhicaryāvatāra)*, translated by Marion L. Matics. London, New York: Macmillan, 1970. Complete English translation, poetic and readable.

55. *A Guide to the Bodhisattva's Way of Life (Bodhicaryāvatāra)*, translated by Stephen Batchelor and Sherpa Tulku. Dharamsala: Library of Tibetan Works and Archives, 1979. Complete English translation. DPB $8.95 (paper)

Kamalaśīla. Bhāvanākrama. *See* The Third Process of Meditative Actualization.

56. *A Lamp for the Path and Commentary by Atīśa*

(Bodhipathā-pradīpa), translated and annotated by Richard Sherburne. Winchester, Mass.: Allen & Unwin, 1983. Details the stages of the Buddhist path; a concise guide for Dharma students. DPB $12.50

57. *Lucid Exposition of the Middle Way,* translated by Mervyn Sprung. Boulder: Prajñā Press, 1979. English translation of 16 chapters of Candrakīrti's Prasannapadā. DPB $35.00

58. "Madhyamārthasaṅgraha of Bhāvaviveka," restored into Sanskrit from the Tibetan and translated by N. Aiyaswami Sastri. *Journal of Oriental Research* 5 (1931):41–49. The nature of the two truths as explained in the Mādhyamika system.

59. *Mahāyānaviṁśaka of Nāgārjuna,* edited and translated by V. Bhattacharyya. Calcutta: Viśva-bharati, 1931. Reconstructed Sanskrit; Tibetan; Chinese; complete English translation.

60. *La Marche à la lumiére: Bodhicaryāvatāra,* a complete French translation by Louis Finot. Paris: Éditions Bossard, 1920. (Les classiques de l'Orient 2).

61. "Nāgārjuna. Mahāyāna-viṁśaka," translated by Susumu Yamaguchi. *Eastern Buddhist* 4 (1927):169–176. Tibetan and Chinese texts with complete English translation.

Nāgārjuna. Mūlamadhyamaka-kārikā. *See below; see also* Conception of Buddhist Nirvana; Emptiness, A Study in Religious Meaning.

62. *Nāgārjuna: A Translation of his Mūlamadhyamaka-kārikā,* by Kenneth K. Inada. Tokyo: Hokuseido Press, 1970. Includes introductory essay useful for students. DPB $29.50

Nāgārjuna. Vigrahavyāvartanī. *See* The Dialectical Method of Nāgārjuna.

63. *Nāgārjuniana: Studies in the Writings and Philosophy of Nāgārjuna,* translations by Christian Lindtner. Copenhagen: Akademisk Forlag, 1982. (Indiske Studier 4). Contains English translations of the Śūnyatāsaptati, Yuktiṣaṣṭikā, Lokātitastava, Acintyastava, Bodhicittavivaraṇa, and the Bodhisambhāra.

64. "Ratnāvalī of Nāgārjuna," translated by G. Tucci. *Journal of the Royal Asiatic Society* (1934):307–325; (1936):237–252, 423–435.

Śāntideva. Bodhicaryāvatāra. *See below; see also* Bodhicaryāvatāra; Entering the Path of Enlightenment; A Guide to the Bodhisattva's Way of Life; La Marche à la lumiére.

65. *Śāntideva: Eintritt in das Leben zur Erleuchtung* (Bodhicaryāvatāra), translated by Ernst Steinkellner. Dusseldorf; Cologne: Eugen Diedrichs, 1981. Complete German translation.

66. "The Third Process of Meditative Actualization by Kamalaśīla," translated by Robert F. Olson and Masao Ichishima. *Taishō Daigaku Sōgō Bukkyō Kenkyūjo Nempō* (1979):241–205.

67. *Tibetan Buddhistology, the Bhāvanākrama of Kamalaśīla,* translated by Shyuki Yoshimura. Kyoto: Research Society for the Eastern Sacred Books, 1953. Contains romanized Tibetan text with Japanese and English translations.

68. *Le Traité de la grande vertu de sagesse de Nāgārjuna (Mahāprajñāpāramitā-śāstra),* translated by

Étienne Lamotte. 5 vols. Louvain: Université de Louvain, Institut Orientaliste, 1949–1980. An authoritative and scholarly translation (incomplete), with much additional information.

Yogācāra

69. *A Buddhist Doctrine of Experience: Works of Vasubandhu,* translated by T. A. Kochmuttom. Delhi: Motilal Banarsidass, 1982. Foundation texts of the Vijñānavādin school.

Asaṅga. Bodhisattvabhūmi. *See* On Knowing Reality.

Asaṅga. Mahāyānasaṁgraha. *See* Le Somme du grand véhicule.

70. *Ch'eng Wei-shih-lun: The Doctrine of Mere-Consciousness,* translated from the Chinese by Wei Tat. Hong Kong: Ch'eng Wei-shih-lun Publications, 1973. Includes translation of Vasubandhu's Viṁśaka and Triṁśikā and their commentaries.

71. *The Madhyānta-Vibhaṅga: Discourse on Discrimination between Middle and Extremes,* translated from the Sanskrit by Th. Stcherbatsky. Reprint of 1936 ed. Calcutta: Indian Studies Past and Present, 1971. A partial translation.

72. *Mahāyānasūtrālaṁkāra: Exposé de la doctrine du grand véhicule selon le système Yogācāra.* Vol. II: Traduction, par Sylvain Lévi. Paris: Champion, 1911. Complete French translation.

Maitreyanātha. Mahāyānottara-tantra. *See* A Study

of the Ratnagotravibhāga; The Sublime Science of the Great Vehicle to Salvation.

73. "The Meditational Therapy of the Madhyānta-vibhāgabhāṣya," by Stephan Anacker, in *Mahāyāna Buddhist Meditation: Theory and Practice.* Honolulu: University of Hawaii Press, 1978. Includes a translation of chapters 2, 4, and part of 5 of Vasubandhu's text. pp. 83–113. DPB $17.50

74. *On Knowing Reality: The Tattvārtha Chapter of Asaṅga's Bodhisattvabhūmi,* translated by Janice Dean Willis. New York: Columbia University Press, 1979. Translation of chapter 4, part 1. DPB $20.00

75. *Readings on Yogācāra Buddhism,* translated by A. K. Chatterjee. Varanasi: Banares Hindu University, 1971.

76. *Le Siddhi de Hsüan-Tsang (Vijñaptimātratāsiddhi),* translated by Louis de la Vallée Poussin. 2 vols. Paris: Paul Geuthner, 1928–1929, 1948. Complete French translation of Vasubandhu's Viṁśaka and Triṁśikā with their commentaries.

77. *A Study on the Ratnagotravibhāga (Uttaratantra),* being a treatise on the Tathāgatagarbha theory of Mahāyāna Buddhism, by Jikido Takasaki. Rome: IsMEO, 1966. (Serie Orientale Roma 33). Includes English translation.

78. *Le Somme du grand véhicule,* translated by Étienne Lamotte. 2 vols. Louvain, 1938–1939. French translation of Asaṅga's Mahāyānasaṁgraha.

79. "The Sublime Science of the Great Vehicle to Salvation, being a Manual of Buddhist Monism: The Work of Ārya Maitreya with a Commentary by

Āryāsaṅga," translated from the Tibetan by E. Obermiller. *Acta Orientalia* 9 (1930):81–306. Reprinted, Shanghai: 1940. Complete English translation of the Mahāyānottaratantra.

80. *The Treatise in Twenty Stanzas on Representation Only*, translated from the Chinese version of Hsüan Tsang by Clarence Hamilton. New Haven: American Oriental Society, 1938. Translation of Vasubandhu's Viṁśaka.

81. *The Trisvabhāva-nirdeśa of Vasubandhu*, Sanskrit text and Tibetan versions with English translation by Sujitkumar Mukhopadhyaya. Calcutta: Viśvabharati, 1939. Contains glossaries.

Vasubandhu. *See* A Buddhist Doctrine of Experience.

82. *Vasubandhu's Karmasiddhiprakaraṇa, Traité de la demonstration de l'acte,* translated by Étienne Lamotte. Brussels, 1935 (Mélanges Chinoises et Bouddhiques 4), pp. 207–263.

83. *Vijñapti-mātratā-siddhi, with Sthiramati's Commentary,* translated by K. Chatterjee. Varanasi, 1980. English translation.

84. *Yogācāra-bhūmi by Saṁgharakṣa,* translated by Paul Demiéville. Paris: Bulletin de l'École Française d'Extrême-Orient 44 (1954):339–436. An early Yogācāra treatise on meditation.

85. "The Yogāvatāropadeśa: A Mahāyāna Treatise on Yoga by Dharmendra," translated by Durgacharan Chatterji. *Journal of the Asiatic Society of Bengal,* n.s. 23 (1927):249–259.

Vasubandhu. Madhyāntavibhāgabhāṣya. *See* The Meditational Therapy of the Madhyāntavibhāga-bhāṣya.

Logic

86. *Ālaṁbāṇaparīkṣā and Vṛtti,* translated by N. Aiyaswami Sastri. Madras: Adyar Library, 1942. (Adyar Library Series 32). Complete Sanskrit ed. restored; complete English translation of Dignāga's text and commentary.

87. *Buddhist Logic,* translated by Th. Stcherbatsky. Reprint of 1930 ed. New York: Dover, 1962. 2 vols., contains a complete English translation of Dharmakīrti's Nyāyabindu. DPB $6.95/vol.

88. *Buddhist Formal Logic,* by R. S. Y. Chi. London: Luzac, 1969. Contains a complete translation of Dignāga's Hetucakra and K'uei-chi's commentary on the Nyāyapraveśa.

89. *The Buddhist Philosophy of Universal Flux.* An exposition of the philosophy of critical realism as expounded by the school of Diṅnāga, by Satkari Mookerjee. Reprint of 1935 ed. Delhi: Motilal Banarsidass, 1980.

90. "Buddhist Solipsism: A Free Translation of Ratnakīrti's Saṃtanantaraduṣana," by Y. Kajiyama. *Indogaku Bukkyōgaku Kenkyū/Journal of Indian and Buddhist Studies* 13 (1965):435–420.

Dharmakīrti. Nyāyabindu. *See* Buddhist Logic.

Dharmakīrti. Pramāṇavārttika. *See* The Pramāṇavārttikam of Dharmakīrti.

Dharmakīrti. Sāmtānāntarasiddhi. *See* Papers of Th. Stcherbatsky.

Dignāga. Hetucakra. *See* Buddhist Formal Logic.

Dignāga. Nyāyamukha. *See* The Nyāyamukha of Dignāga.

Dignāga. Pramāṇasamuccaya. *See* Dignāga. On Perception.

91. *Dignāga. On Perception,* by Masaaki Hattori. Cambridge, Mass.: Harvard University Press, 1968. Translation of the Pratyakṣapariccheda of Dignāga's Pramāṇasamuccaya.

92. *Early Buddhist Theory of Knowledge,* by J. N. Jayatilleke. London: Allen & Unwin, 1963. Excellent advanced study.

93. *An Eleventh Century Buddhist Logic of 'Exists', Ratnakīrti's Kṣanabhaṅga-siddhi Vyātirekātmikā,* edited and translated by Charlene McDermott. Dordrecht, Netherlands: Reidel, 1970.

94. *The Nyāyamukha of Dignāga: The Oldest Buddhist Text on Logic after Chinese and Tibetan Materials,* translated by G. Tucci. Reprint of 1930 ed. San Francisco: Chinese Materials Center, 1976.

95. *Papers of Th. Stcherbatsky,* translated by Harish C. Gupta. Calcutta: Indian Studies Past & Present, 1969. Contains free translations of Dharmakīrti's Saṁtānāntarasiddhi and Vinītadeva's Saṁtānāntarasiddhiṭīkā.

96. *The Pramāṇavārttikam of Dharmakīrti (First Chapter with Commentary)*, translated by Raniero Gnoli. Rome: IsMEO, 1969. (Serie Orientale Roma 23).

97. *Pre-Dignāga Buddhist Texts on Logic from Chinese Sources,* translated by G. Tucci. Reprint of 1929 ed. San Francisco: Chinese Materials Center, 1976.

Ratnakīrti. Kṣanabhaṅgasiddhi-vyatirekātmikā. *See* An Eleventh Century Buddhist Logic of 'Exists'.

Ratnakīrti. Saṁtānāntaradūṣaṇa. *See* Buddhist Solipsism.

Ratnakīrti. Sthirasiddhidūṣaṇa. *See below.*

98. *La Refutation Bouddhique de la Permanence des Choses,* translated by Katsumi Mimaki. Paris: Boccard, 1976. French translations of Ratnakīrti's Sthirasiddhidūṣaṇa, pp.83–181, and Dharmottara's Kṣaṇabhaṅgasiddhi.

Śāntarakṣita. Tattvasaṅgraha. *See* The Tattvasaṅgraha of Śāntarakṣita.

99. *The Tattvasaṅgraha of Śāntarakṣita with the Commentary of Kamalaśīla,* translated by Ganganatha Jha. 2 vols. Baroda: Oriental Institute, 1937–1939. (Gaekwad's Oriental Series 81, 83).

100. *Vinītadeva's Nyāyabinduṭīkā,* translated by M. Gangopadhyaya. Calcutta: Indian Studies Past and Present, 1971.

Vinītadeva. Sāmtānāntarasiddhi-ṭīkā. *See* Papers of Th. Stcherbatsky.

Birth Stories, Poetry, Letters, and Epics

Āryaśūra. Jātakamālā. *See* The Marvelous Companion (Jātakamālā): Life Stories of the Buddha.

101. "The Aṣṭamahāsthāna-caityastotra and the Chinese & Tibetan Versions of a Text Similar to It," translated by Hajime Nakamura. *Indianisme et Bouddhisme: Mélanges offerts à Mgr. Étienne Lamotte,* pp. 259–262. Louvain: Institut Orientaliste Louvain-la-Neuve, 1980. English translation.

Aśvaghoṣa. Buddhacarita. *See* Buddhacarita.

Aśvaghoṣa. Saundarananda. *See* Saundarananda.

102. *The Awakening of Faith, attributed to Asvaghosha,* the essentials of Mahāyāna Buddhism. Translated, with commentary by Yoshito S. Hakeda. New York: Columbia University Press, 1967. An introductory Mahāyāna teaching. DPB $7.50

103. *Buddhacarita, or Acts of the Buddha.* Complete Sanskrit text with English translation by E. H. Johnston, from the work of Aśvaghoṣa. Delhi: Motilal Banarsidass, 1972. English translation of cantos 1–14. Cantos 15-28 translated in "The Buddha's Mission and Last Journey," *Acta Orientalia* 15 (1956):26–62, 85–111, 231–292.

104. "Buddha-Karita of Ashvaghosha," translated by E. B. Cowell. *Buddhist Mahāyāna Texts,* part II, edited by F. Max Müller. Reprint ed. New York: Dover, 1969. English translation of cantos 1–17.

105. *Golden Zephyr. Nāgārjuna: A Letter to a Friend (Suḥrllekha),* translated from the Tibetan by Leslie Kawamura. Berkeley: Dharma Publishing, 1975. A

translation of Mi-pham's "Garland of White Lotus Flowers," a commentary with Nāgārjuna's text.

DPB $6.50

106. *The Marvelous Companion (Jātakamālā): Life Stories of the Buddha, by Āryaśūra.* Berkeley: Dharma Publishing, 1983. A readable modern translation, recommended for beginning students.

DPB $25.00

107. *Minor Buddhist Texts,* translated by G. Tucci. Reprint ed. Delhi: Motilal Banarsidass, 1975.

Nāgārjuna. Suhṛllekha. *See* Golden Zephyr; Nāgārjuna's Letter to King Gautamīputra.

108. *Nāgārjuna's Letter to King Gautamīputra (Suhṛllekha),* with explanatory notes based on Tibetan commentaries, translated from the Tibetan by Lozang Jamspal. Delhi: Motilal Banarsidass, 1978. Complete English translation.

109. *The Royal Song of Saraha: A Study in the History of Buddhist Thought,* translated by Herbert V. Guenther. Seattle: University of Washington Press, 1969.

Śāntideva. Śikṣāsamuccaya. *See* Shiksha-samuccaya.

Saraha. Dohās. *See* Royal Song of Saraha.

110. *The Saundarananda of Asvaghosa,* Sanskrit text with English translation by E. H. Johnston. Delhi: Motilal Banarsidass, 1975. A Buddhist drama by an outstanding poet, one of the few preserved to modern times.

111. *Shikshā-samuccaya: A Compendium of Buddhist Doctrine compiled by Śāntideva,* translated from the Sanskrit by Cecil Bendall and W. H. D. Rouse. Reprint of 1922 ed. Delhi: Motilal Banarsidass, 1981.

Pāli Texts

Vinaya

112. *The Book of the Discipline (Vinaya),* translated by I. B. Horner. 6 vols. London: The Pali Text Society, 1966–1982.

Sutta

113. Dīgha-nikāya. *Dialogues of the Buddha,* translated by T. W. and C. A. F. Rhys-Davids. 3 vols. Reprint ed. London: Pali Text Society, 1977. The 34 longer suttas.

114. Majjhima Nikāya. *The Middle Length Sayings,* translated by I. B. Horner. Reprint ed. London: Pali Text Society, 1975–1977. The 152 medium-length suttas.

115. Saṁyutta-nikāya. *The Book of the Kindred Sayings,* translated by C. A. F. Rhys-Davids and F. L. Woodward. 5 vols. Reprint ed. London: The Pali Text Society, 1975–1982. The 2,889 shorter suttas, grouped into five major sections.

116. Anguttara-nikāya. *The Book of the Gradual Sayings,* translated by F. L. Woodward and E. M. Hare. 5 vols. Reprint ed. London: The Pali Text Society, 1972–1982. A collection of 2,308 suttas.

117. Khuddakapāṭha. *The Minor Readings and Illustrator,* translated by Bhikkhu Ñāṇamoli. Reprint ed. London: Pali Text Society, 1978. The first book of the Khuddaka-nikāya with its commentary.

118. *Dhammapada,* translated by S. Radhakrishnan. Oxford: The University Press, 1959. New York: Penguin, 1983. The second book of the Khuddaka-nikāya.

119. *Dhammapada, Wisdom of the Buddha,* translated by Harischandra Kaviratna. Los Angeles: Theosophical University Press, 1980. DPB $5.95

120. *The Minor Anthologies of the Pali Canon,* translated by I. B. Horner and H. S. Gehman. Reprint ed. London: The Pali text Society, 1974. Contains books of the Khuddaka-nikāya: Part II, the Udāna and the Itivuttaka, the third and fourth books; part III, the Buddhavaṁsa and the Cariyāpiṭaka, the fourteenth and fifteen books; part IV, Vimānavatthu amd Petavatthu, the sixth and seventh books.

121. *Verses of Uplift (Itivuttaka): As It Was Said,* translated by F. L. Woodward. London: Pali Text Society, 1948. Collection of short discourses in prose and verse.

122. *The Elders' Verses,* translated by K. R. Norman. 2 vols. London: Pali Text Society, 1969, 1971. Prose translation of the Theragātha and Therīgātha, the eighth and ninth books of the Khuddaka-nikāya. Also translated by C. A. F. Rhys-Davids, *Psalms of the Early Buddhists* (Verse Translation). Reprint ed. London: Pali Text Society, 1980.

123. *Jataka Stories,* translated by various hands under the editorship of E. B. Cowell. 3 vols. Reprint ed. London: The Pali Text Society, 1981. The tenth book of the Khuddaka-nikāya.

124. *The Path of Discrimination (Paṭisaṁbhidāmagga),* translated by Bhikkhu Ñāṇamoli. London: Pali Text Society, 1970. The twelfth book of the Khuddaka nikāya.

125. *The Piṭaka disclosure (Peṭakopadeśa),* translated by Bhikkhu Ñāṇamoli. Reprint ed. London: Pali Text

Society, 1979. The sixteenth book of the Khuddakanikāya.

126. *The Guide (Netti-pakaraṇam),* translated by Bhikkhu Ñāṇamoli. London: Pali Text Society, 1977. Considered the seventeenth book of the Khuddakanikāya in the Burmese tradition.

127. *Milinda's Questions (Milindapañha),* translated by I. B. Horner. 2 vols. London: Pali Text Society, 1969. Considered the eighteenth book of the Khuddakanikāya in the Burmese tradition.

128. *The Book of Protection,* translated by Thera Piyatissa. Kandy, 1975. A collection of 24 suttas, often considered a supplement to the Suttapiṭaka.

Abhidhamma

129. Dhammasaṅgani. *Buddhist Psychological Ethics,* translated by C. A. F. Rhys-Davids. 3rd ed. London: The Pali Text Society, 1974. The first book of the Abhidhamma-piṭaka.

130. Vibhaṅga. *The Book of Analysis,* by U. Thittila. London: Pali Text Society, 1969. The second book of the Abhidhamma-piṭaka.

131. Dhātukathā. *Discourse on Elements,* translated by U. Nārada. London: Pali Text Society, 1962. The third book of the Abhidhamma-piṭaka.

132. Puggala-Paññatti. *Designation of Human Types,* translated by B. C. Law. London: Pali Text Society, 1979. Abhidhamma treatise on the concept of 'person'. The fourth book of the Abhidhammapiṭaka.

133. Kathāvatthu. *Points of Controversy*, translated by S. Z. Aung and C. A. F. Rhys-Davids. London: H. Milford, 1915. The fifth book of the Abhidhamma-piṭaka.

134. Paṭṭhāna. *Conditional Relations*, translated by U. Nārada. London: Pali Text Society, 1981. The seventh book of the Abhidhamma-piṭaka.

Commentaries, Manuals, and Later Works

135. *Abhidhammattha Saṅgaha of Anuruddhācariya*, edited in the original Pāli text with English translation and notes by Nārada Mahāthera. Kandy: Buddhist Publication Society, 1968.

136. *Buddhist Legends*, translated by E. W. Burlingame. 3 vols. Reprint of 1921 ed. London: Pāli Text Society, 1979. Traditional commentary on the Dhammapada.

137. *The Chronicle of the Thūpa and the Thūpavaṁsa*, being a translation and edition of Vācissaratthera's Thūpavaṁsa, by N. N. Jayawickrama. London: The Pali Text Society, 1971.

138. *Clarifier of the Sweet Meaning (Buddhavaṁsa Commentary)*, translated by I. B. Horner. London: Pali Text Society, 1978.

139. *Compendium of Philosophy (Abhidhammattha-saṅgaha)*, translated by S. Z. Aung and C. A. F. Rhys-Davids. Reprint of 1910 ed. London: Pali Text Society, 1979. A Theravāda text on Abhidhamma with an informative introduction and notes.

140. *The Debates Commentary (Kathāvatthu Commentary)*, translated by B. C. Law. 1940. Reprint 1969.

141. *The Expositor*, translated by Pe Maung Tin. 2 vols. Reprint ed. London: Pali Text Society, 1971. Translation of the Atthasālinī, the commentary on the Dhammasaṅgani.

142. *Inception of Discipline*, translation by N. A. Jayawickrama. London: Pali Text Society, 1962.

143. *A Manual of Abhidhamma*, Pāli text and translation of the Abhidhammattha Saṅgaha, with explanatory notes by Narada Mahathera. Kandy: Buddhist Publication Society, 1981.

144. *The Path of Purification (Visuddhimagga), by Buddhaghosa*, translated from the Pali by Bhikkhu Nyānamoli. Reprint ed. Berkeley: Shambhala, 1976. A commentary on the three aspects of the teachings: śīla, samādhi, prajñā, or virtue, concentrative meditation, and wisdom.

145. *The Perfect Generosity of Prince Vessantara*, translated from the Pāli by Margaret Cone and Richard F. Gombrich. New York: Oxford University Press, 1977. The oldest extant version of a Buddhist epic, illustrated with previously unpublished paintings from Sinhalese temples.

146. *Peta-Stories (Petavatthu Commentary)*, translated by U Ba Kyaw and P. Masefield. London: Pali Text Society, 1980.

147. *The Sheaf of Garlands of Epochs of the Conqueror (Jinakālamālī)*, translated by N. A. Jayawickrama. London: Pali Text Society, 1968.

148. *The Sūtra on the Foundation of the Buddhist Order*, vol. I, translated by Ria Kloppenborg. Leiden: E. J. Brill, 1973.

149. *Tales and Teachings of the Buddha: The Jataka Stories in Relation to the Pali Canon*, by John Garrett Jones. London: Allen & Unwin, 1979. Includes notes, bibliography, and index.

Books on Buddhism

India

Biography

150. Abhayadatta. *Buddha's Lions: The Lives of the Eighty-four Siddhas (the Caturaśīti-siddha-pravṛtti),* translated by James Robinson. Berkeley: Dharma Publishing, 1979. (Tibetan Translation Series 10). DPB $16.95

151. *Buddha and the Gospel of Buddhism,* by Ananda Coomaraswamy. New York: Harper & Row, 1964.

152. *The Life and Teaching of Nāropa,* translated from the original Tibetan by Herbert V. Guenther. Reprint ed. Oxford: University Press, 1971. An engrossing account of Nāropa's study and practice under his guru, the great siddha Tilopa.

153. *The Life of the Buddha as Legend and History,* by E. J. Thomas. London: Routledge and Kegan Paul, 1960.

Geography

154. Cunningham, Alexander. *The Ancient Geography of India, vol. I: The Buddhist Period.* Reprint ed. Varanasi: Indological Book House, 1963.

155. Law, B. C. *Geography of Early Buddhism.* Reprint of 1932 ed. New Delhi: Oriental Books, 1979.

156. Sircar, D. C. *Studies in the Geography of Ancient and Medieval India.* 2nd ed. revised and enlarged. Delhi: Motilal Banarsidass, 1971.

History and Culture

157. Bapat, P. V. *2500 Years of Buddhism.* New Delhi:

Publications Division, Ministry of Information and Broadcasting, Government of India, 1956.

158. *Les Sectes bouddhiques du Petit Véhicule,* translated by André Bareau. Saigon: École Française d'Extrême-Orient, 1955.

159. Barua, Depak Kumar. *Viharas in Ancient India: A Survey of Buddhist Monasteries.* Calcutta, 1969.

160. Basham, A. K. *The Wonder That Was India.* New York: Grove Press, 1959. An excellent overview of Indian history and culture.

161. Bu-ston Rin-chen grub. *History of Buddhism (Chos-'byung),* translated by E. Obermiller. Leipzig: Reprint Series, Heidelburg, 1931. Part 1, The Jewelery of Scripture; part 2, The History of Buddhism in India and Tibet. An excellent primary source for doctrinal summaries and overview of Buddhist history.

162. Dutt, Nalinaksha. *Buddhist Sects in India.* Delhi: Motilal Banarsidass, 1978. Describes the early Sangha and the historical context of its development, with overview of doctrinal development.

163. Dutt, Nalinaksha. *Early Monastic Buddhism.* Calcutta: Mukhopadhyay, 1971.

164. Fa-hien. *Record of Buddhistic Kingdoms: An Account of his Travels in India and Ceylon (A.D. 399-414),* translated by James Legge. Reprint ed. New York: Dover, 1965. DPB $3.00

165. *History and Culture of the Indian People.* R. C. Majumdar, general editor. 11 vols. London: George Allen & Unwin; Bombay: Bharatiya Vidya Bhavan, 1951-1969. A detailed and authoritative history. Most volumes have been reprinted.

166. Hsüan-tsang. *Buddhist Records of the Western World,* translated from the Chinese by Samuel Beal. Reprint of 1884 edition. Delhi: Motilal Banarsidass, 1981. DPB $30.00

167. I-tsing. *A Record of the Buddhist Religion as Practised in India and the Malay Archipelago (A.D.671–695),* translated by J. Takakusu. 2nd Indian ed. New Delhi: Munshiram Manoharlal, 1982.

168. Joshi, Lal Mani. *Studies in the Buddhistic Culture of India (7th and 8th c. A.D.).* 2nd rev. ed. Delhi: Motilal Banarsidass, 1977. DPB $19.00

169. Lamotte, Étienne. *Histoire du bouddhisme indien.* Louvain: Publications universitaires, 1958. An excellent history of Buddhism from the earliest times to the close of the Saka era.

170. *The Mahāvastu,* translated by J. J. Jones. 3 vols. Reprint ed. London: Pali Text Society, 1973–1978. (Sacred Books of the Buddhists 16, 18, 19). A traditional chronicle of the northern Buddhist tradition. Contains most of the history and legends relating to the Buddha that were current at the time it was compiled.

171. Nakamura, Hajime. *Indian Buddhism: A Survey with Bibliographical Notes.* Hirakata City, Japan: KUFS Publication, 1980. (Intercultural Research Institute Monograph 9). Contains extensive bibliographical notations and indexes.

172. Nakamura, Hajime. "The Coming into Existence of Mahāyāna Sūtras," *Bulletin of the Okurayama Oriental Research Institute* 2 (1957).

173. Narain, A. K., ed. *Studies in the History of Buddhism.* Delhi: B. R. Publishing Corp., 1980. Contains essays and articles by well-known scholars and teachers.

174. Rahula, Walpola. *The Heritage of the Bhikkhu.* New York: Grove Press, 1974. "A short history of the Bhikkhu in educational, cultural, and political life."

175. Saddhamma-Saṅgaha. *A Manual of Buddhist Historical Traditions,* translated by B. C. Law. Delhi: Bharatiya Publishers, 1980.

176. Tāranātha. *Tāranātha's History of Buddhism in India,* translated from the Tibetan by Lama Chimpa and Alaka Chattopadhyaya; edited by D. P. Chattopadhyaya. Calcutta: K. P. Bagchi, 1980.

177. Warder, A. K. *Indian Buddhism.* 2nd rev.ed. Delhi: Motilal Banarsidass, 1980. Includes bibliography, 46 pp. DPB $25.00

178. Winternitz, M. *A History of Indian Literature.* Vol. II, *Buddhist Literature and Jaina.* Reprint of 1933 ed. Delhi: Motilal Banarsidass, 1983.

Sri Lanka

179. *Culavaṁsa,* being the more recent part of the Mahāvaṁsa, part 1, translated by Wilhelm Geiger. London: Pali Text Society, 1973.

180. Evers, Hans-Dieter. *Monks, Priests, and Peasants: A Study of Buddhism and Social Structure in Central Ceylon.* Leiden: Brill, 1972.

181. Geiger, Wilhelm. "Pāli Literature," chapter I of *Pāli Literature and Language.* Calcutta: University of Calcutta, 1943. pp. 1–59.

182. Gombrich, Richard F. *Precept and Practice: Traditional Buddhism in the Rural Highlands of Ceylon.* London: Oxford University Press, 1971.

183. *The Great Chronicle of Ceylon (Mahāvaṁsa),* translated by Wilhelm Geiger. Reprint of 1912 ed. London: Pali Text Society, 1980.

184. Ludowyk, E. F. C. *The Footprint of the Buddha.* London: Allen & Unwin, 1958. Description of the monuments of ancient Ceylon.

185. Law, B. C. A *History of Pali Literature.* London: Kegan Paul, Trübner, 1933. Reprint forthcoming from AMS Press, 1984.

186. Rahula, Walpola. *History of Buddhism in Ceylon: The Anurādha Period (3rd c. B.C.–10th c. A.D.).* Colombo: M. D. Guna Sena & Co., 1956.

187. Smith, Bardwell L., ed. *The Two Wheels of Dhamma.* Chambersburg, PA: American Academy of Religion, 1972. A helpful study on Sri Lankan Buddhism.

Kashmir, Ladakh, and Nepal

188. Francke, A. H. *Antiquities of Indian Tibet.* 2 vols. Reprint ed. New Delhi: S. Chand & Co., 1972. vol. I, Personal Narrative; vol. II, Chronicles of Ladakh. Texts and translations with notes and maps. First published 1926.

189. Harvey, Andrew. *A Journey in Ladakh.* New York: Houghton Mifflin, 1984 (paperback ed.). A very personal account of a modern-day pilgrim and his journey of discovery. DPB $8.95

190. Kalhaṇa. *Kalhaṇa's Rājataraṅginī; A Chronicle of the Kings of Kaśmir,* translated by M. A. Stein. 2 vols. Reprint ed. Delhi: Motilal Banarsidass, 1979.

191. Macdonald, Alexander W. "The Writing of Buddhist History in the Sherpa Area of Nepal." *Studies in the History of Buddhism,* by A. K. Narain. Delhi: B. R. Publishing Corp, 1980. pp.121-132.

192. Naudou, Jean. *Buddhists of Kaśmir,* translated from the French by Brereton and Picron. 1st English ed. Delhi: Agam Kala Prakashan, 1980. A good survey, particularly useful for translation history of Tibetan canonical texts. Describes Kashmiri-Tibetan relationships during the 1st and 2nd transmissions.

193. Petech, Luciano. *The Kingdom of Ladakh, c.950–1842 A.D.* Rome: IsMEO, 1977. (Serie Orientale Roma 51).

194. Ram, Rajendra. *A History of Buddhism in Nepal: A.D.704–1396.* Delhi: Motilal Banarsidass, 1978.

195. Rowell, Galen. *Many People Come, Looking, Looking.* Seattle: The Mountaineers, 1980. Rowell, a mountain-climber, photographer, and writer, has put together a readable, beautiful book on the Himalayan region. DPB $30.00

196. Snellgrove, D. L. and Skorupski, T. *The Cultural Heritage of Ladakh.* 2 vols. Warminster, England: Aris & Phillips, 1977, 1980.

197. Tsering, Nawang. *Buddhism in Ladakh.* New Delhi: Sterling Publishers, 1979. A study of the life and works of the eighteenth century Ladakhi Saint and Scholar Grub-chen Ngag-dbang Tse-ring, from a 2 volume autobiography, edited by a disciple, Tshul-khrims 'byung-gnas.

Central Asia

198. Harmatta, J. *Prolegomena to the Sources on the History of Pre-Islamic Central Asia.* Budapest: Akadémiai Kiado, 1979. Examination of Greek, Latin, Byzantine, Old Iranian, Middle Iranian, Old Indian, Aramaic, Syrian, Arabic, Chinese, and Tibetan sources, as well as numismatic and archaeological sources, by experts in these areas. Articles in English, German, and French.

199. Saha, Kshanika. *Buddhism and Buddhist Literature in Central Asia.* Calcutta: Mukhopadhyay, 1970.

200. Stein, Sir Aurel. *On Ancient Central-Asian Tracks. Brief Narrative of Three Expeditions in Innermost Asia and Northwestern China.* Reprint ed. New York: Pantheon, 1964. An unusual and readable account, describing "the most daring and adventurous raid upon the ancient world that any archaeologist has attempted."

201. Stein, Sir Aurel. *Serindia.* 5 vols. Reprint ed. Delhi: Motilal Banarsidass, 1980–1982. Detailed report of explorations carried out in Central Asia and Westernmost China during the years 1906–1908. Includes plates, unusually finely detailed maps, and appendices; contains information on artifacts and manuscripts.

202. Waley, Arthur. *Ballads and Stories from Tun-huang.* London: George Allen & Unwin, 1960.

China

Biography

203. *The Life of Hiuen-tsiang, by the Shaman Hwui Li,* translated by Samuel Beal. New edition. London: Kegan Paul, Trench, Trübner, & Co., 1911. A biography of the famous 7th century Chinese pilgrim and translator.

Philosophy and Schools

204. Chang, Garma C. C. *The Buddhist Teaching of Totality: The Philosophy of Hua-yen Buddhism.* University Park: Pennsylvania State University Press, 1971. Includes translation of portions of the Avataṁsaka-sūtra. DPB $10.95

205. Ch'eng, Hsüeh-li. *Empty Logic: Mādhyamika Buddhism from Chinese Sources.* New York: Philosophical Library, 1984. An aid to understanding the important doctrine of emptiness, with bibliography, glossary, index. DPB $17.95

206. *Chinese Buddhist Verse,* translated by Richard H. Robinson. London: John Murray, 1955.

207. Cleary, Thomas. *Entry into the Inconceivable: An Introduction to Hua-yen Buddhism.* Honolulu: University of Hawaii Press, 1983. Includes translations of five Hua-yen treatises. DPB $16.95

208. Cook, Francis H. *Hua-yen Buddhism: The Jewel Net of Indra.* University Park: Pennsylvania State University Press, 1977. Includes notes, glossary, index. DPB $16.95

209. Park, Sung-bae. *Buddhist Faith and Sudden Enlightenment.* Albany: SUNY Press, 1983. Methods of mind cultivation from the Hua-yen, Pure Land, and the Ch'an schools. DPB $8.95

210. *The Platform Sutra of the Sixth Patriarch,* translated by Philip B. Yampolsky. New York: Columbia University Press, 1967. A major scripture of the Ch'an (Zen) school; the text of the Tun-huang manuscript in a scholarly translation.

211. *Studies in Ch'an and Hua-yen,* edited by Robert M. Gimello and Peter M. Gregory. Honolulu: University of Hawaii Press, 1984. (The Kuroda Institute, Studies in East Asian Buddhism 1). Includes chapter, "Early Ch'an Schools in Tibet." DPB $14.95

212. Thompson, Laurence G. *Chinese Religion: An Introduction.* 3rd ed. Belmont, CA: Wadsworth, 1980.

213. Welch, Holmes. *The Practice of Chinese Buddhism.* Cambridge, Mass.: Harvard University Press, 1967. Interviews with Ch'an monks; a scholarly and readable work.

History and Culture

214. Ch'en, Kenneth. *Buddhism in China: A Historical Survey.* New York: Princeton University Press, 1964. Reprinted (paper), 1972, 1973. DPB $7.95

215. Ch'en, Kenneth. *The Chinese Transformation of Buddhism.* Princeton: Princeton University Press, 1973. DPB $9.50

216. *Ennin's Travels in T'ang China,* translated by Edwin Reischauer. New York: The Ronald Press, 1955.

217. Chiu T'ang-shu. *The History of Early Relations between China and Tibet,* translated from the

Chinese by Don Y. Lee. Bloomington, Indiana: Eastern Press, 1981. Useful resource for the T'ang period (7th to 9th centuries); corresponds with the introduction of Buddhism to Tibet.

218. *One Hundred Poems from the Chinese,* translated by Kenneth Rexroth. New York: New Directions, 1971. A fine little collection; some appear for the first time in English. With introduction and notes. DPB $4.95

219. Pachow, W. *Chinese Buddhism: Aspects of Interaction and Reinterpretation.* Lanham, Md.: University of America Press, 1980. Includes comparative study of Lao Tzu and Gautama Buddha. DPB $14.95

220. Wright, Arthur F. *Buddhism in Chinese History.* Stanford: Stanford University Press, 1974.

221. Zurcher, E. *The Buddhist Conquest of China: The Spread and Adaptation of Buddhism in Early Medieval China.* 2 vols. Reprint of 1959 edition. Leiden: E.J. Brill, 1972. Vol. I, text; vol. II, notes, bibliography, and indexes.

Japan and Korea

Works by Japanese Masters

222. Bankei. *The Unborn: The Life and Teaching of Zen Master Bankei, 1622–1693,* translated by Norman Waddell. San Francisco: North Point Press, 1984. DPB $11.25

223. *Buddhist Culture in Korea,* edited by the International Cultural Foundation. Seoul: The Si-sa-yon-o-sa Publishers, 1983.

224. Dōgen. *How to Raise an Ox,* translations from the

writings of Dōgen by Francis H. Cook. Los Angeles: Center Publications, 1979. Dōgen was the founder of the Sōtō Zen school. DPB $7.95

225. *Kukai: Major Works,* translated, with an account of his life and a study of his thought by Yoshito S. Hakeda. New York: Columbia University Press, 1972. Important study of the founder of Shingon Buddhism. DPB $16.95

226. *Lives of Eminent Korean Monks,* translated by Peter H. Lee. Cambridge, Mass.: Harvard University Press, 1969. A collection of traditional biographies.

227. *Miraculous Tales of the Lotus Sutra from Ancient Japan: The Dainikonkoku Hokekyōkenki of Priest Chingen,* translated and annotated by Yoshiko K. Dykstra. Honolulu: University of Hawaii Press, 1983.

228. Ryōkan. *One Robe, One Bowl: The Zen Poetry of Ryōkan,* translated by John Stevens. New York: Weatherhill, 1983. DPB $4.95

229. Soyen Shaku. *Sermons of a Buddhist Abbot.* New York: Samuel Weiser, 1971.

History and Culture

230. *Bashō: The Narrow Road to the Deep North and Other Travel Sketches,* translated by Nobuyuki Yuasa. Baltimore: Penguin, 1966. A classic account of the travels of one of Japan's most famous poets, a master of the Haiku form.

231. De Bary, W. M. Theodore, ed. *Sources of the Japanese Tradition.* New York: Columbia University Press, 1958.

232. Kiyota, Minoru. *Shingon Buddhism: Theory and

Practice. Los Angeles: Buddhist Books International, 1978. Includes annotated bibliography and glossary of technical terms. DPB $6.95

233. Matsunaga, Daigan and Alicia. *The Foundation of Japanese Buddhism*. 2 vols. Los Angeles: Buddhist Books International, 1974, 1976.

234. *One Hundred Poems from the Japanese*, translated by Kenneth Rexroth. New York: New Directions, 1964. Introduction gives background on the history and nature of Japanese poetry; includes bibliography. DPB $4.95

235. Steinilber-Oberlin, Emile. *The Buddhist Sects of Japan: Their History, Philosophical Doctrines, and Sanctuaries*. Westport: Greenwood Press, 1976.

236. Suzuki, D. T. *Zen and Japanese Culture*. Princeton: Princeton University Press, 1973. DPB $9.95

237. *T'ien-t'ai Buddhism: An Outline of the Fourfold Teachings*, edited by David W. Chappell and compiled by Masao Ichishima. Honolulu: University of Hawaii Press, 1983.

Tibet

Writings of the Masters

238. *Āryaśūra's Aspiration*, with a commentary by Gendun Gyatso, the Second Dalai Lama, and *A Meditation on Compassion*, from a discourse by His Holiness the Fourteenth Dalai Lama, together with a sādhana of Avalokiteśvara, translated and edited by Brian C. Beresford with I. T. Doboom Tulku, Gonsar Tulku, and Sherpa Tulku. Dharamsala: Library of Tibetan Works and Archives, 1981. DPB $5.95

Bu-ston Rin-chen grub. De-bzhin gsegs-pa'i snying-po gsal-zhing mdzes-par byed-pa'i rgyan. *See* Le Traité du Tathāgatagarbha.

239. *The Diamond Light of the Eastern Dawn.* A Collection of Tibetan Buddhist Meditations, translated by Janice Dean Willis. New York: Simon & Schuster, 1972.

240. sGam-po-pa. *The Jewel Ornament of Liberation,* translated and annotated by H. V. Guenther. Boulder: Prajñā Press, 1981. A Tibetan manual of preparation and the path, important for Dharma students. DPB $12.50

241. The Lama Lodro of Drepung. *The Prince Who Became a Cuckoo: A Tale of Liberation,* translated and edited by the Lama Geshe Wangyal. New York: Theater Arts Books, 1982. DPB $6.95

242. Longchenpa. *Kindly Bent to Ease Us,* translated by H. V. Guenther. 3 vols. Berkeley: Dharma Publishing, 1975–1976. Very valuable and poetic description of the Bodhisattva path by one of the most revered Nyingma masters of all time. DPB $7.95 (vol. I); $6.50 (vol. II); $6.50 (vol. III).

243. Padmasambhava. *Tibetan Book of the Dead (Bardo Thodol),* translated by Francesca Fremantle and Chogyam Trungpa. Boulder: Shambhala, 1975.

244. *The Precious Garland and the Song of the Four Mindfulnesses,* translated by Jeffrey Hopkins and Lati Rinpoche. New York: Harper & Row, 1975. The seventh Dalai Lama's commentary on a text by Nāgārjuna. DPB $5.95

245. Sa-skya Paṇḍita. *Elegant Sayings.* Sakya Paṇḍita's commentary, with Nāgārjuna's root verses. Berkeley: Dharma Publishing, 1973. DPB $5.95

246. Sa-skya Paṇḍita. *A Treasury of Aphoristic Jewels: The Subhāṣita-ratnanidhi of Sakya Paṇḍita,* translated by James E. Bosson. Bloomington: Indiana University, 1969. Tibetan and Mongolian Texts with English translation.

247. *Spiritual Guide to the Jewel Island,* by Konchog Tanpa Donme, translated by Blanche C. Olschak and Thupten Wangyal. Zurich: Buddhist Publications, Institute for Buddhist Psychology and Central Asian Studies, 1973. Trilingual edition: Tibetan, English, and German. DPB $7.95

248. *Le Traité du Tathāgatagarbha de Bu Ston Rin chen grub,* translated by David Seyfort Ruegg. Paris: École Française d'Extrême Orient, 1973. Includes bibliographical references and indexes.

249. Tenzin Gyatsho, Fourteenth Dalai Lama. *The Key to Mādhyamika,* translated by Gonsar Tulku, with the assistance of Gavin Kilty. Dharamsala: Library of Tibetan Works & Archives, 1974.

250. Tenzin Gyatsho, Fourteenth Dalai Lama. *The Opening of the Wisdom Eye and the History of the Advancement of the Buddhadharma in Tibet.* Wheaton, Ill.: Theosophical Publishing House, 1981. DPB $5.75

251. Tsong-kha-pa. *Calming the Mind and Discerning the Real.* Buddhist meditation and the middle view, from the Lam Rim Chenmo of Tsong-kha-pa, translated by Alex Wayman. New York: Columbia University Press, 1978. A partial translation; includes bibliography and index. A Tibetan approach to mental development. DPB $40.00

252. Tsong-kha-pa. *The Yoga of Tibet: The Great Exposition of Secret Mantra,* edited and translated by Jeffrey Hopkins. Boston: Allen & Unwin, 1981. DPB $13.50

253. *Tsong Khapa's Speech of Gold in the Essence of True Eloquence: Reason and Enlightenment in the Central Philosophy of Tibet,* translated by Robert A. F. Thurman. Princeton: Princeton University Press, 1984. Includes glossary of technical terms, bibliography, and index. DPB $50.00

254. Ye-shes rgyal-mtshan. *Mind in Buddhist Psychology,* translated by Herbert V. Guenther and Leslie S. Kawamura. Berkeley: Dharma Publishing, 1975. A translation of an Abhidharma commentary, "The Necklace of Clear Understanding," by the 18th century master Ye-shes rgyal-mtshan. Based on Asaṅga's Abhidharmasamuccaya and other traditional texts. DPB $6.50

Biography

255. *Atīśa and Tibet: Life and Works of Dīpaṁkara Śrījñāna in Relation to the History and Religion of Tibet,* translated by Lama Chimpa. Calcutta: Indian Studies Past and Present, 1967.

256. *Biography of Dharmasvāmi,* translated by George Roerich. Patna: K. P. Jayaswal R. I., 1959.

257. *Four Lamas of Dolpo,* translated by David L. Snellgrove. 2 vols. Oxford: Bruno Cassierer, 1967. Vol. I, introduction and translations; vol. II, Tibetan texts and commentaries.

258. *The Legend of the Great Stupa and the Life Story of the Lotus Born Guru.* Berkeley: Dharma Publishing, 1973. DPB $6.50

259. *The Life and Liberation of Padmasambhava,* by Yeshe Tsogyal, translated by Kenneth Douglas and Gwendolyn Bayes. 2 vols. Berkeley: Dharma Publishing, 1977. An important gter-ma text. Padmasambhava, born in Oḍḍiyāna, was extremely important to the early transmission of the Dharma in Tibet; Yeshe Tsogyal was one of his closest disciples. A fine edition, illustrated with full-color plates of Tibetan paintings. DPB $55.00 (set of 2 vols., cloth)

260. *The Life of Bu Ston Rinpoche, with Tibetan Text of the Bu Ston rNam thar, translated by D. S. Ruegg.* Rome: IsMEO, 1966. (Serie Orientale Roma 34)

261. *The Life of Marpa the Translator: Seeing Accomplishes All,* by Tsang Nyon Heruka. Translated from the Tibetan by the Nālandā Translation Committee under the direction of Chogyam Trungpa. Boulder: Prajñā Press, 1982. DPB $10.00

262. *The Life of Milarepa,* translated by Lobsang P. Lhalungpa. New York: Dutton, 1977; Boulder: Great Eastern, 1982. A new translation. DPB $8.95

263. *Mother of Knowledge: The Enlightenment of Ye-shes mTsho-rgyal,* by Nam-mkha'i snying-po. Translated by Tarthang Tulku and Jane Wilhelms. Berkeley: Dharma Publishing, 1983. DPB $21.95

264. *My Land and My People: The Autobiography of His Holiness, The Dalai Lama,* by Tenzin Gyatsho, the Fourteenth Dalai Lama. New York: Potala, 1979. DPB $6.95

265. *Tibet's Great Yogi Milarepa,* A Biography from the Tibetan, being the Jetsun-kaḥbum or biographical history of the great saint of Tibet, Milarepa, acording to Lama Kazi-Dawa-Samdup's English rendering.

Edited by W. Y. Evans-Wentz. London: Oxford University Press, 1928. Reprinted 1980. DPB $6.95

266. *Women of Wisdom,* by Tsultrim Allione. Boston: Routledge & Kegan Paul, 1984. A biographical account of six Tibetan women 'saints' or yoginīs, from the 11th through the 20th centuries; a tribute to the spiritual power of women. DPB $12.95

Schools, Meditation, Philosophy

267. An-che, Li. *Rñin-ma-pa: The Early Form of Lamaism.* London: Royal Asiatic Society, 1948. Xerox copies available. DPB $1.00

268. Blofeld, John. *The Tantric Mysticism of Tibet: A Practical Guide to the Theory, Purpose, and Techniques of Tantric Meditation.* Reprint ed. Boulder: Prajñā Press, 1982. DPB $9.00

269. Dargyay, Eva M. *The Rise of Esoteric Buddhism in Tibet.* New York: Samuel Weiser, 1978. Part 1, a study of the origins of the rNying-ma-pa school; part 2, a translation of the 6th chapter of bDud-'joms Rinpoche's "Rise of the Old School," containing biographies of the great gter-stons of Tibet. DPB $7.95

270. *Four Essential Buddhist Texts.* 1st rev.ed. Dharamsala: Library of Tibetan Works and Archives, 1982. Includes "The Opening of the Dharma," by 'Jam-dbyangs mKhyen-brtse Chos-kyi blo-'gros, an overview of the doctrines and practices of the major traditions; "The Foundation of Buddhist Meditation," by Kalu Rinpoche; "The Great Seal of Voidness," by the First Panchen Lama; and "A Key to the Madhyamaka," by His Holiness the Fourteenth Dalai Lama.

271. Govinda, Lama Anagarika. *Creative Meditation and Multi-dimensional Consciousness*, Wheaton, Ill.: Theosophical Publishing House, 1976. DPB $8.50

272. Govinda, Lama Anagarika. *Foundations of Tibetan Buddhism According to the Esoteric Teachings of the Great Mantra: Om Mani Padme Hum*. York Beach, Maine: Weiser, 1982. DPB $7.95

273. Guenther, Herbert V. *Tibetan Buddhism in Western Perspective*. Berkeley: Dharma Publishing, 1977. DPB $6.95

274. Hoffman, Helmut. *The Religions of Tibet*. London: Allen & Unwin, 1961. A useful overview.

275. Karma Thinley, Lama Wangchim. *The History of the Sixteen Karmapas of Tibet*. Boulder: Prajñā Press, 1980. DPB $6.95

276. Tulku Thondup. *Buddhist Civilization in Tibet*. Maha Siddha Nyingmapa Center. Conway, Mass., 1982. Concise outline of the Tibetan Buddhist schools, their history, major teachers, texts, teachings, and principal monasteries. DPB $9.95

277. Tucci, Giuseppe. *The Religions of Tibet*, translated from the German and Italian by Geoffrey Samuel. Berkeley: University of California Press, 1980. Fully detailed descriptions of the Buddhist schools. DPB $21.95

Geography

278. Rockhill, W. Woodville. *Tibet. A Geographical, Ethnographical, and Historical Sketch derived from Chinese Sources*. An extract from the Journal of the Royal Asiatic Society of Great Britain and Ireland. 1891, reprinted Peking, 1939.

279. *The Geography of Tibet, according to the Dzam gling rgyas bshad,* translated by Turrell Wylie. Rome: IsMEO, 1962. A primary text, helpful for understanding Tibetan culture.

History and Culture

280. Choephel, Gedun. *The White Annals,* translated from the Tibetan by Samten Norboo. Dharamsala: Library of Tibetan Works and Archives, 1978. DPB $4.95

281. Demiéville, Paul. *Le Concile de Lhasa.* Paris: Presses Univérsitaires de France, 1952. An authoritative survey of the debate between Indian and Chinese Buddhists in 8th century Tibet.

282. Ekvall, Robert. *Religious Observances in Tibet: Pattern and Function.* Chicago: University of Chicago Press, 1964.

283. Gold, Peter. *Tibetan Reflections: Life in a Tibetan Refugee Community.* London: Wisdom Publications, 1984. A bright and enjoyable book; includes photographs by the author and illustrations by Tibetan artists. DPB $11.95

284. Gos lo-tsā-ba gZhon-nu dpal. *The Blue Annals: The Stages of the Appearance of the Doctrine and Preachers in the Land of Tibet,* translated by George N. Roerich. Delhi: Motilal Banarsidass, 1979. Valuable primary reference source for students of Tibetan Buddhist History. For place name index, *see* no. 309. DPB $40.00

285. Govinda, Li Gotami. *Tibet in Pictures.* 2 vols. Berkeley: Dharma Publishing, 1979. A photographic record of an expedition to Central and Western

Tibet; a moving account of a lost world and its sacred works of art. DPB $50.00

286. Haarh, Erik. *The Yar-Lun Dynasty.* Copenhagen: G. E. C. Gad's Forlag, 1969. "A study with particular regard to the contribution by myths and legends to the history of ancient Tibet and the origin and nature of its kings."

287. Harrar, Heinrich. *Seven Years in Tibet.* Reprint of 1953 ed. Los Angeles: J. P. Tarcher, 1982. A true adventure of a German national in Tibet during World War II. Informative and interesting. DPB $8.95

288. Hoffman, Helmut. *Tibet: A Handbook.* London: George Allen & Unwin, 1961. A concise and informative reference for students.

289. Jigmei, Ngapo Ngawang, and others. *Tibet.* New York: McGraw-Hill, 1981. An extensive documentation of Tibet, its history, palaces, customs, religion, monasteries, and art. Many full-color plates.

290. Khosla, Romi. *Buddhist Monasteries in the Western Himalaya.* Kathmandu: Ratna Pustak Bhandar, 1979. Contains many color photographs, architectural plans, and drawings.

291. Lhalungpa, Lobsang P. *Tibet: The Sacred Realm.* New York: Aperture, 1983. A photographic history of the years 1880–1950.

292. Michael, Franz, and Knez, Eugene. *Rule by Incarnation: Tibetan Buddhism & Its Role in Society & State.* Boulder: Westview, 1982.

293. Miller, Beatrice D. "Views of Women's Roles in Buddhist Tibet." *Studies in the History of Buddhism,*

by A. K. Narain. Delhi: B. R. Publishing Corp, 1980. pp.155–166.

294. Mkhyen-brtse. *Mk'yen brtse's Guide to the Holy Places of Central Tibet.* translated by Alfonsa Ferrari, completed by L. Petech. Rome: Istituto Italiano per il Medio ed Estremo Oriente, 1958. (Serie Orientale Roma 16)

295. Norbu, Thubten Jigme, and Turnbull, Colin. *Tibet: Its History, Religion, and People.* New York: Simon & Schuster, 1968.

296. Pathak, Suniti Kumar. *The Indian Nītiśāstras in Tibet.* Delhi: Motilal Banarsidass, 1974. DPB $6.00

297. Pelliot, Paul, tr. *Histoire ancienne du Tibet.* Paris: Librairie d'Amérique et d'Orient. Adrien-Maisonneuve, 1961. (Oeuvres posthumes de Paul Pelliot 5). Translations from the T'ang Annals.

298. Shakabpa, Tsepon W. D. *Tibet: A Political History.* New Haven: Yale University Press, 1967. An excellent source of historical information.

299. Sinha, Nirmal Chandra. *Tibet: Considerations on Inner Asian History.* Calcutta: Mukhopadhyaya, 1967. DPB $4.95

300. Snellgrove, David L. and Richardson, Hugh. *A Cultural History of Tibet.* Reprint of 1968 edition. Boulder: Prajñā, 1980. DPB $12.50

301. bSod-nams grags-pa. *Deb t'er dmar po gsar ma: Tibetan Chronicles,* translated from the Tibetan by G. Tucci. Roma: IsMEO, 1971. (Serie Orientale Roma 24). Tibetan text and English translation.

302. Stein, R. A. *Tibetan Civilization.* Stanford: Stanford

University Press, 1972. Useful survey, recommended for students. DPB $7.95

303. *The Superhuman Life of Gesar of Ling*, related by Alexandra David-Neel and the Lama Yongden. translated with the collaboration of Violet Sydney. Boulder: Prajñā Press, 1981. The epic of Gesar reflects the spirit of the Tibetan people. DPB $9.00

304. Teichman, Eric. *Travels of a Consular Officer in Eastern Tibet, together with a History of the Relations between China, Tibet, and India.* Cambridge: University Press, 1922.

305. *Tibetan Studies in Honour of Hugh Richardson*, edited by Michael Aris and Aung San Suu Kyi. Proceedings of the International Seminar of Tibetan Studies, Oxford 1979. Warminster, England: Aris & Phillips Ltd., 1980. Collection of articles on many subjects by western scholars.

306. Tucci, Giuseppe. *Trans-Himalaya.* Geneva: Nagel Publishers, 1973. A readable account of the author's travels.

307. Vostrikov, A. I. *Tibetan Historical Literature*, translated from the Russian by Harish Chandra Gupta. Calcutta: Indian Studies Past and Present, 1970. (Soviet Indology Series 4). Important study of Tibetan language and culture.

308. Wayman, Alex. "Observations on the History and Influence of the Buddhist Tantra in India and Tibet." *Studies in the History of Buddhism*, by A. K. Narain. Delhi: B. R. Publishing Corp., 1980. pp. 359–364.

309. Wylie, Turrell V. *A Place Name Index to George N. Roerich's Translation of the Blue Annals.* Rome:

IsMEO, 1957. (Serie Orientale Roma 15). An indispensible index for this valuable resource.

Tibetan Medicine

310. *Tibetan Medicine,* illustrated in original texts, presented and translated by Ven. Rechung Rinpoche. Berkeley: University of California Press, 1976. Includes a translation of the biography of the Elder gYu-thog Yon-tan mGon-po, the famous court physician of King Khri-srong lde-btsan (eighth century). Includes glossary and index of medical topics.
DPB $11.95

311. *Tibetan Medicine, with Special Reference to Yoga Śataka,* by Bhagwan Dash. Dharamsala: Library of Tibetan Works & Archives, 1976. Contains key Tibetan medical terms and prescriptions, with Sanskrit equivalents.

Southeast Asia

312. Coedès, G. *The Indianized States of Southeast Asia,* translated by Susan Brown Cowing. Honolulu: University Press of Hawaii, 1968. A history of Cambodia.

313. King, Winston L. *A Thousand Lives Away: Buddhism in Contemporary Burma.* Cambridge, Mass: Harvard University Press, 1964.

314. Spiro, Melford E. *Buddhism and Society: A Great Tradition and its Burmese Vicissitudes.* New York: Harper & Row, 1971.

315. *Three Worlds According to King Ruang: A Thai Buddhist Cosmology,* translated by Frank E. Rey-

nolds and Mani B. Reynolds. Berkeley: Asian Humanities Press, 1982. Includes charts, notes, glossary, and index. DPB $30.00

316. *The Wheel of the Law, Illustrated from Siamese Sources by the Modern Buddhist.* A life of Buddha and an account of the Phrabat, translated by Henry Alabaster. Westmead, England: Gregg International Publishers, 1971.

Anthologies

317. *Buddhism: A Religion of Infinite Compassion*, edited by Clarence Hamilton. Indianapolis: Bobbs-Merrill, 1952.

318. *Buddhism in Translations*, translated by Henry Clarke Warren. New York: Atheneum, 1963. Selections from the Pāli suttas.

319. *A Buddhist Bible*, edited by Dwight Goddard. Reprint ed. New York: Beacon, 1970. DPB $10.75

320. *The Buddhist Experience: Sources and Interpretations*, by Stephan Beyer. Belmont, CA: Wadsworth Publishing, 1974. DPB $10.95

321. *Buddhist Suttas*, translated by T. W. Rhys-Davids. New York: Dover Publications, 1969. Includes the Mahāparinibbana and other suttas from the Theravāda tradition.

322. *Buddhist Texts Through the Ages*, edited by Edward Conze. New York: Harper & Row, 1964. Translations from Pāli, Sanskrit, Apabhramsa, Tibetan, and Japanese. DPB $8.95

323. *The Buddhist Tradition in India, China, and Japan*, edited by W. M. Theodore de Bary. New York: Random House, 1972. An anthology of texts from the three major traditions. DPB $3.95

324. *The Perfection of Wisdom: The Career of the Predestined Buddhas*. A selection of Mahāyāna scriptures translated from the Sanskrit by E. J. Thomas. Reprint of 1952 ed. Westport, Conn: Greenwood Press, 1979.

325. *The Teachings of the Compassionate Buddha*, edited by E. A. Burtt. New York: New American Library,

1982. Contains selections from the Śūraṅgama Sūtra, the Saddharmapuṇḍarīka Sūtra, and the Laṅkāvatāra Sūtra. DPB $2.50

326. *The Wisdom Gone Beyond: An Anthology of Buddhist Texts*. Bangkok: Social Science Association Press, 1966.

327. *Women in Buddhism: Images of the Feminine in the Mahāyāna Tradition*, by Diana Y. Paul. Berkeley: Asian Humanities Press, 1979. Includes translations of passages concerning women drawn from Mahāyāna Sūtras. DPB $19.00

General Introductory Readings: Foundation and Practice

328. *Bodhisattva of Compassion: The Mystical Tradition of Kuan Yin*, by John Blofeld. Boulder: Shambhala, 1978. A clear and readable expression of the Buddhist view of compassion. DPB $5.95

329. *Buddhism: A Modern Perspective*, edited by Charles S. Prebish. University Park: Pennsylvania State University Press, 1978. Outlines of the main points of the major themes and traditions of Buddhism; each section contains useful suggestions for further reading. DPB $10.95

330. *Buddhism: Its Essence and Development*, by Edward Conze. Reprint ed. New York: Harper & Row, 1975. A useful summary of Buddhist doctrines emphasized by the major traditions. DPB $5.95

331. *Buddhism, Its Origin and Spread in Words, Maps, and Pictures*. Leiden: Brill, 1959. American ed. New York: St. Martin's Press, 1962. Helpful for following

the progress of Buddhism in India and throughout all of Asia.

332. *The Buddhist Religion: A Historical Introduction,* by Richard Robinson and Willard L. Johnson. 3rd ed. Belmont, CA: Wadsworth Publishing, 1982. An overview of Buddhist teachings and the spread of Buddhism in Asia. A helpful survey and reference for the major traditions. DPB $10.95

333. Conze, Edward. *Buddhist Thought in India: Three Phases of Buddhist Philosophy.* Ann Arbor: University of Michigan Press, 1970. An introductory work on Buddhist teachings. DPB $6.95

334. *Calm and Clear,* a traditional meditation text translated from the Tibetan by Tarthang Tulku. Berkeley: Dharma Publishing, 1973. A basic text for meditation classes at the Nyingma Institute. DPB $6.50

335. *Crystal Mirror,* edited by Tarthang Tulku. Berkeley: Dharma Publishing, 1972– . A series devoted to introducing the Buddhist teachings to western students. Vols. II-VII available: vol. II, $4.95; vol. III, $5.95; vol. IV, $9.95; vol. V-VII, $12.95.

Contents: Vol. II-III: The essential teachings and practices, with articles on Buddhist psychology and philosophy. Vol. IV: Articles on the early history of Buddhism in Tibet from traditional sources; Tibetan culture; the essential teachings and their practice. Vol V: An integrated survey, including the life of the Buddha and the history of the Sangha in India, with emphasis on the lineages transmitted to Tibet. Vol. VI: A more comprehensive presentation of the Buddha, Dharma and Sangha, with a survey of

Dharma transmission in Tibet and other Asian lands. Vol. VII: More historically oriented; includes 35 maps and timelines, with chapters on the transmission of the texts and the development of the Buddhist Canons of the northern and southern traditions. Includes information on Buddhism in the West and the state of Dharma transmission today.

336. *The Door of Liberation: Essential Teachings of the Tibetan Buddhist Tradition,* by Geshe Wangyal. Boulder: Shambhala, 1983. A helpful introductory text by a master of the Gelug tradition; includes translations from traditional teachings. DPB $7.95

337. *Entering the Path of Enlightenment,* translated by Marion L. Matics. New York: Macmillan, 1970. A readable translation of the Bodhicaryāvatāra, a poetic and inspiring description of the Bodhisattva path by the great master Śāntideva.

338. *The Experience of Insight,* by Joseph Goldstein. Boulder: Shambhala, 1983. A simple and direct guide to Buddhist meditation as practiced in the Theravada tradition; basic to all forms of Buddhist practice. DPB $6.95

339. *Gesar.* Dharma Publishing's quarterly publication, containing introductory articles on Buddhism for the general reader. DPB $10.00/4 issues

340. *Gesture of Balance,* by Tarthang Tulku. Berkeley: Dharma Publishing, 1975. A basic orientation to meditation and self-healing for all westerners, by a modern master of the Nyingma tradition. DPB $6.95

341. *Golden Zephyr,* translated by Leslie Kawamura.

Berkeley: Dharma Publishing, 1975. Translation of Mi-pham's commentary on Nāgārjuna's Suhṛllekha, or 'Letter to a Friend', with Nāgārjuna's original verses. A valuable introduction to the Mahāyāna view, expressed in clear, non-technical language.

DPB $6.50

342. *Gotama Buddha,* by Hajime Nakamura. Los Angeles: Buddhist Books International, 1977. The Life of the Buddha and summary of the basic teachings.

DPB $7.95

343. *Hidden Mind of Freedom,* by Tarthang Tulku. Berkeley: Dharma Publishing, 1981. Based upon articles published in *Gesar* and *Crystal Mirror,* explaining basic Buddhist views and practices.

DPB $6.50

344. *The Jewel Ornament of Liberation by sGam-po-pa,* translated by Herbert V. Guenther. Reprint ed. Berkeley: Shambala, 1971. An essential guide for students, beginning with the motive and basis of Dharma study and practice to the training in the six perfections and the five paths to enlightenment, culminating in perfect Buddhahood. sGam-po-pa, disciple of Milarepa, was the founding father of the bKa'-brgyud school of Tibetan Buddhism.

DPB $12.50

345. *Light of Asia, or The Great Renunciation,* being the life and teaching of Gautama, prince of India and founder of Buddhism. Boston: Roberts Bros., 1879. Reprint ed. London: Routledge & Kegan Paul, 1964. Based on the Lalitavistara-sūtra, but not always technically accurate; still an inspiring and poetic work that conveys the spirit of the text.

346. *Kum Nye Relaxation,* by Tarthang Tulku. 2 vols. Berkeley: Dharma Publishing, 1978. Vol. I, theory, preparation, massage; vol. II, movement exercises. Healing exercises to balance and integrate energies of body and mind, based on traditional Tibetan medical practice. Illustrated and clearly explained; valuable for everyone. DPB $7.50/vol.

347. *Mahāyāna Way to Buddhahood: Theology of Enlightenment,* by Susumu Yamaguchi. Translated and edited by Buddhist Books International. Los Angeles, 1982. Concise and very readable work by a Japanese scholar; intended to communicate the basics of Buddhist philosophy to westerners.

348. *The Manual of Insight (Vipassanā Dīpani),* translated by U. Nyana Mahathera from Ledi Sayadaw. Sri Lanka: Buddhist Publication Society, 1975. A guide for the meditation practice known as Vipassanā, basic to all meditation systems, by a leading master of the Theravāda tradition.

349. *On Zen Practice,* edited by Hakuyu Taisan Maizumi and Bernard Tetsugen Glassman. Los Angeles: Zen Center of Los Angeles, 1976. A manual of meditation and practical aspects of Zen teachings.

350. *Openness Mind,* by Tarthang Tulku. Berkeley: Dharma Publishing, 1978. Complements *Gesture of Balance;* includes more advanced practices useful for gaining insight into the nature of mind. DPB $6.50

351. *Outlines of Mahayana Buddhism,* by D. T. Suzuki. New York: Schloken Books, 1963. An introductory work, useful for students.

352. *Reflections of Mind,* edited by Tarthang Tulku. Berkeley: Dharma Publishing, 1975. Collection of essays on Tibetan and western approaches to the study of mind. Useful background for western Dharma students. DPB 6.95

353. *Selected Sayings from the Perfection of Wisdom,* chosen, arranged, and translated by Edward Conze. Reprint ed. Boulder: Prajñā Press, 1978. Passages from the Prajñāpāramitā, essential texts of the second turning teaching and the heart of Mahāyāna Buddhism. Inspirational and supportive. DPB $5.95

354. A *Short History of Buddhism,* by Edward Conze. London: Allen & Unwin, 1981. A brief overview that can be read at one sitting; useful historical orientation for beginners. DPB $10.95

355. *Skillful Means,* by Tarthang Tulku. Berkeley: Dharma Publishing, 1978. Practical application of Buddhist attitudes to everyday work situations; work as an opportunity for self-knowledge and growth. DPB $6.50

356. *A Survey of Buddhism,* by Sangharaksita. Boulder: Shambhala, 1980. An introductory work, useful for beginners. DPB $10.95

357. *Theravada Meditation: The Buddhist Transformation of Yoga,* by Winston L. King. University Park: Pennsylvania State University Press, 1980. "The first book in English to relate modern forms of Theravāda meditational practice to its Indian roots." DPB $17.95

358. *The Three Jewels,* by Sangharakṣita. Reprint ed. London: Windhorse Publications, 1977. A readable

overview of the meaning of Buddha, Dharma, and Sangha by an English bhikkhu ordained in the Theravāda tradition. Valuable introduction to Buddhist views and the concept of compassion. DPB $5.95

359. *Tibet's Great Yogi Milarepa,* A Biography from the Tibetan, being the Jetsun-kaḥbum or biographical history of the great saint of Tibet, Milarepa, according to Lama Kazi-Dawa-Samdup's English rendering. Edited by W. Y. Evans-Wentz. London: Oxford University Press, 1928. Reprinted 1980. An inspiring account of the life of Tibet's great yogi and saint; conveys the spirit of devotion that insures success in Dharma practice. DPB $8.95

360. *The Voice of the Buddha: The Beauty of Compassion.* 2 vols. Berkeley: Dharma Publishing, 1983. The first complete English translation of the Lalitavistara Sūtra, the Buddha's own account of his life, enlightenment, and first teaching, expressed in free verse and poetic prose. An essential reading for all Dharma students; a fine edition of the life of Śākyamuni Buddha, illustrated with traditional Tibetan thankas. DPB $55.00/boxed set

361. *Way of the White Clouds,* by Lama Anagarika Govinda. Boulder: Shambhala, 1970. An inspirational account of a pilgrimage to Tibet by a westerner who became a well-known master and writer on Tibetan Buddhism and symbology. DPB $9.95

362. *What the Buddha Taught,* by Walpola Rahula. Revised and expanded ed. New York: Grove Press, 1983. A clear statement of the essential Buddhist teachings of the four truths and the nature of the

path; includes translations of the Buddha's teachings preserved in the southern (Theravāda) tradition. DPB $6.95

363. *The Wheel of Life: Autobiography of a Western Buddhist,* by John Blofeld. Berkeley: Shambhala, 1972. Informative and inspiring account of personal experience of the teachings, distilled from a lifetime of study, practice, and devotion.

364. *The World of Buddhism. Buddhist Monks and Nuns in Society and Culture.* Heinz Bechert and Richard Gombrich, eds. New York: Facts on File, Inc., 1984. Readable and authoritative descriptions and historical surveys, including the state of Buddhism today in traditional lands and in the West. Contains essays by Étienne Lamotte, Eric Zurcher, Per Kvaerne, and others, in addition to those by the editors. Includes 82 color plates, 215 photographs, drawings and maps. DPB $49.95

365. *Zen is Eternal Life,* by Jiyu Kennett. Berkeley: Dharma Publishing, 1976. Formerly entitled *Selling Water by the River,* this new edition restores Kennett Roshi's original expression of the Sōtō Zen teachings. A manual of Zen training, including excerpts from traditional masters. DPB $10.95

366. *Zen Mind, Beginner's Mind,* by Shunryu Suzuki, edited by Trudy Dixson. New York: Weatherhill, 1974. A gem of a book, a clear expression of the beauty of humility and simplicity, by a Zen master of the Sōtō tradition who introduced Zen practice to many westerners. DPB $5.00

367. *Zen Philosophy, Zen Practice,* by Thich Thien-An. Berkeley: Dharma Publishing, 1975. A readable

introduction to the theoretical and practical aspects of Zen by a Vietnamese Zen master; includes meditation practices which reinforce the topic of each chapter. DPB $6.50

Modern Works on Vinaya

368. *Recherches sur la Biographie du Buddha dans les Sūtrapiṭaka et les Vinayapiṭaka anciens,* translated by André Bareau. 2 vols. Paris: École Française d'Extrême-Orient, 1970–1971. French text.

369. *Earliest Vinaya and the Beginnings of Buddhist Literature,* by Erich Frauwallner. Rome: IsMEO, 1956. (Serie Orientale Roma 8) Helpful analysis and comparison of the Vinaya texts of the early schools.

Modern Works on Buddhist Psychology

370. *Abhidhamma Papers,* edited by Mark Rowlands. Manchester, England: The Samatha Trust, 1982.

371. *The Birth of Indian Psychology and its Development in Buddhism,* by C. A. F. Rhys-Davids. Reprint of 1936 ed. New Delhi: Oriental Books, 1978.

372. *The Central Conception of Buddhism and the Word 'Dharma',* by Th. Stcherbatsky. Delhi: Motilal Banarsidass, 1974. DPB $7.50

373. *The Dynamic Psychology of Early Buddhism,* by R. E. A. Johansson. London: Curzon, 1979.

374. *The Early Buddhist Theory of Man Perfected,* a study of the Arahanī concept and of the implication of the aim to perfection in religious life. Traced in early

canonical and post-canonical Pāli literature by I. B. Horner. Amsterdam: Philo Press, 1975.

375. *Faith and Knowledge in Early Buddhism,* an analysis of the contextual structures of an arahant-formula in the Majjhima-Nikāya, by Jan T. Ergardt. Leiden: Brill, 1977.

376. *Guide Through the Abhidhamma,* a synopsis of the seven books of the Abhidhamma Canon, followed by an essay on dependent origination, by Nyanatiloka Mahāthera. Kandy: Buddhist Publication Society, 1980.

377. *Mind in Buddhist Psychology,* translated by Herbert V. Guenther and Leslie S. Kawamura. Berkeley: Dharma Publishing, 1975. A translation of an Abhidharma commentary, "The Necklace of Clear Understanding," by the 18th century master Ye-shes rgyal-mtshan. Based on Asaṅga's Abhidharmasamuccaya and other traditional texts. DPB $6.50

378. *The Paccekabuddha: A Buddhist Ascetic,* a study of the concept of the paccekabuddha in Pāli canonical and commentarial literature, by Ria Kloppenborg. Leiden: Brill, 1974.

379. *Philosophy and Psychology in the Abhidharma,* by Herbert V. Guenther. Berkeley: Shambhala, 1976.

380. *The Psychological Attitude of Early Buddhist Philosophy and its Systematic Representation According to Abhidhamma Tradition,* by Lama Anagarika Govinda. New York: Samuel Weiser, 1974.

Modern Works on Buddhist Philosophy

381. "Bhāvaviveka and the Prāsaṅgika School," by Yuichi Kajiyama. *Nava Nālandā Mahāvīhara Research Publications*, vol. 1, pp. 289–331.

382. *The Bodhisattva Doctrine in Buddhist Sanskrit Literature*, by Har Dayal. Reprint of 1932 ed. New York: Samuel Weiser, 1978. DPB $10.00

383. *Buddhist Causality: The Central Philosophy of Buddhism*, by David J. Kalupahana. Honolulu: University of Hawaii Press, 1975. DPB $14.00

384. *The Buddhist Nirvana and its Western Interpreters*, by Guy Welbon. Chicago: University of Chicago Press, 1968.

385. *Buddhist Philosophy: An Historical Analysis*, by David J. Kalupahana. Honolulu: University of Hawaii Press, 1976. DPB $4.95

386. *Buddhist Philosophy in Theory and Practice*, by Herbert V. Guenther. Baltimore, Maryland: Penguin Books Inc., n.d. Includes translations of two Tibetan works explaining the four philosophical schools, by masters of the Gelug and Nyingma traditions.

387. *Buddhist Thought in India: Three Phases of Buddhist Philosophy*, by Edward Conze. Ann Arbor: University of Michigan Press, 1970. DPB $6.95

388. *Buddhist Studies, 1924–1972*, by Edward Conze. San Francisco: Zen Center, 1967–1975. A valuable collection of articles and book reviews by an acknowledged scholar. DPB 20.00

389. *Early Mādhyamika in India and China*, by Richard H. Robinson. Reprint ed. New York: Samuel Weiser, 1978. A good standard work. DPB $6.95

390. *The Essentials of Buddhist Philosophy,* by Junjiro Takakusu. New York: Samuel Weiser, 1978. Discusses the different schools of Buddhism, with emphasis on the Japanese developments.

DPB $6.95

391. *History of Buddhist Thought: Early Buddhist Thought According to the Pāli Canon* by E. J. Thomas. London: Routledge, Kegan Paul, 1971. Contains appendix and bibliography.

392. *An Introduction to Buddhist Philosophy,* by Yuichi Kajiyama. Kyoto, 1966. (Memoirs of the Faculty of Letters, Kyoto University, 10). An annotated translation of Mokṣākaragupta's Tarkabhāṣa.

393. *Meditation on Emptiness,* by Jeffrey Hopkins. London: Wisdom Publications, 1984. An explication of Buddhist philosophy, with an exposition of the Prāsaṅgika-Mādhyamika view. Includes translations from traditional sources, with charts, appendices, bibliography, and Tibetan text. Also with English/Sanskrit/Tibetan glossary. DPB $35.00

394. *Prajñāpāramitā and Related Systems: Studies in Honour of Edward Conze,* edited by Lewis Lancaster. Berkeley: Regents of the University of California, 1977. (Berkeley Buddhist Studies Series)

DPB $20.00

395. *Studies in the Laṅkāvatāra,* by D. T. Suzuki. Reprint of 1930 ed. Boulder: Prajñā Press, 1981.

DPB $12.50

396. *A Source Book of Indian Philosophy,* edited by S. Radhakrishnan and Charles Moore. Princeton: Princeton University Press, 1957.

397. *A Study of Vasubandhu's Treatise on the Pure Land,*

with special reference to his theory of salvation in the light of the development of the Bodhisattva ideal, by H. Kimura. M.A. thesis, University of London, 1977.

398. *The Yogācāra Idealism,* translated by A. K. Chatterjee. 2nd rev. ed. Delhi: Motilal Banarsidass, 1975.

Sacred Art

399. *The Art of Central Asia Series. The Stein Collection in the British Museum.* Roderick Whitfield, ed. New York: Kodansha, 1983. Vols. I-II, Paintings from Dunhuang. A collectors item, elegant and expensive.

400. *Art of the Lotus Sutra,* edited by Bunsaku Kurata and Yoshiro Tamura. Tokyo: Kosei Publishing, 1983. Japanese masterpieces; text outlines history and influence of the Lotus Sutra (Saddharmapuṇḍarīka)

401. *Art of Tibet.* Berkeley: University of California Press, 1984. A catalogue of the Los Angeles County Museum of Art by Pratapaditya Pal. A valuable guide to Tibetan art; includes appendix, glossary, and bibliography. DPB $22.50

402. *Arts of Asia.* Kowloon, Hong Kong: Arts of Asia Publications Ltd. A high-quality journal of Asian art; bimonthly. Subscription available through DPB.

403. *Barabuḍur: History and Significance of a Buddhist Monument,* edited by Luis O. Gomez and Hiram W. Woodward, Jr. Berkeley, 1981. (Berkeley Buddhist Studies Series 2)

404. Bernet Kempers, A. J. *Ancient Indonesian Art.* Amsterdam: C. P. J. van der Peet, 1959.

405. Bhattacharyya, B. *The Indian Buddhist Iconography.* 2nd ed. Calcutta: Mukhopadhyaya, 1958. Largely based on the Sādhanamālā.

406. Cunningham, Sir Alexander. *The Bhilsa Topes: The Buddhist Monuments of Central India.* Reprint ed. Varanasi: Indological Book House, 1966.

407. Bryner, E. *Thirteen Tibetan Thankas: The Buddhist Birth Stories.* Colorado, 1958.

408. Bussagli, M. *La Peinture de l'Asie centrale.* Geneva, 1963.

409. Campbell, Joseph. *The Mythic Image.* Princeton: Princeton University Press, 1982. (Bollingen Series C) A feast for the eye; descriptive illustrated text. Includes notes and index. DPB $19.95

410. *Catalogue of the Newark Museum Tibetan Collection.* Vol.I, by Valrae Reynolds. Newark: The Newark Museum, 1983. Originally published in 1950, this work has been completely rewritten and revised. A useful reference for students of Tibetan culture. DPB $11.95

411. Clark, Walter Eugene. *Two Lamaistic Pantheons.* Edited from materials collected by the late Baron A. von Stael-Holstein. Originally published in 2 vols., Cambridge, Mass.: Harvard University Press, 1937; reprint ed. 1 vol., New York: Paragon, 1965. Contains Sanskrit, Tibetan, and Chinese indexes; part II contains plates.

412. Dagyab, Loden Sherap. *Tibetan Religious Art.* 2 vols. Wiesbaden: Harrassowitz, 1977. (Asiatische Forschungen 52).

413. Dehejia, Vidya. *Early Buddhist Rock Temples: A Chronology*. Ithaca: Cornell University Press, 1972.

414. *Dieux et demons du l'Himalaya: Art du Bouddhisme lamaique*, edited by D. G. Beguin and others. Paris: Éditions des Musées Nationaux, 1977. French text, fine color plates.

415. *5000 Years of Korean Art*. René-yvon Lefebvre d'Argencé, general editor. San Francisco: Asian Art Museum of San Francisco, 1979. Catalogue for an exhibition organized by the National Museum of Korea. Includes maps, chronology, and bibliography.

416. Foucher, A. *The Beginnings of Buddhist Art and Other Essays in Indian and Central-Asian Archaeology*. London: Humphrey Milford, 1917.

417. Gaulier, Simone, Jera-Bezard, Robert, and Maillard, Monique. *Buddhism in Afghanistan and Central Asia*. 2 vols. Leiden: E. J. Brill, 1976.

418. Getty, Alice. *The Gods of Northern Buddhism*. Rutland, Vt.: Tuttle, 1977. DPB $39.95

419. Gordon, Antoinette K. *The Iconography of Tibetan Lamaism*. New York: Paragon Book Gallery, 1972.

420. Gordon, Antoinette K. *Tibetan Religious Art*. 2nd ed. New York: Paragon, 1963.

421. Govinda, Lama Anagarika. *Psychocosmic Symbolism of the Buddhist Stupa*. Berkeley: Dharma Publishing, 1976. DPB $6.50

422. Gray, B., and Vincent, J. B., *Buddhist Cave Paintings at Tunhuang*. London, 1959.

423. Griswold, Alexander B., Kim, Chewon, and Pott, Peter H. *The Art of Burma, Korea, and Tibet.* New York: Crown Publishers, 1964. Many color plates.

424. Hallade, Madelaine. *Gandharan Art of North India and the Graeco-Buddhist Tradition in India, Persia, and Central Asia.* 1968.

425. Hisamatsu, Shin'ichi. *Zen Buddhism and its Art.* Kyoto, 1958. Contains 290 plates.

426. Huntington, J. C. *The Phur-ba: Tibetan Ritual Daggers.* Ascona, Switzerland: Artibus Asiae, 1975. Excellent plates with descriptive texts.

427. Lad, P. M. *The Way of the Buddha.* New Delhi: Government of India Publications Division, 1956.

428. Lauf, Detlef-Ingo. *Secret Revelation of Tibetan Thangkas.* Germany: Aurum Verlag GmbH & Co. KG, 1976. Based on the John Gilmore Ford Collection. Text in English and German. DPB $40.00

429. Lauf, Detlef-Ingo. *Tibetan Sacred Art: The Heritage of Tantra.* Boulder: Shambhala, 1976. Now out of print; available in libraries.

430. Liebert, Gösta. *Iconographical Dictionary of the Indian Religions: Hinduism, Buddhism, Jainism.* Leiden: Brill, 1976.

431. *Light of Asia: Buddha Sakyamuni in Asian Art,* organized by Pratapaditya Pal. Los Angeles: Los Angeles County Museum of Art, 1984. An exhibition catalogue with bibliography and index.

432. Marshall, John. *The Buddhist Art of Gandhara: The Story of the Early School, its Birth, Growth, and Decline.* 1960.

433. *The Newark Museum Catalogue of the Tibetan Collection and Other Lamaist Articles.* 5 vols. Newark: Newark Museum, 1971. Completely Revised ed. Vol. I reprinted 1983; vols. II-IV forthcoming. DPB $11.95/vol.

434. Okazaki, Joji. *Pure Land Buddhist Painting,* translated by Elizabeth ten Grotenhuis. Tokyo: Kodansha, 1977. Includes glossary, bibliography, and index.

435. Olschak, Blanche C., in collaboration with Geshe Thubten Wangyal. *Mystic Art of Ancient Tibet.* London, 1973.

436. *Orientations.* A monthly magazine on Asian art for connoiseurs and collectors. Hong Kong. A high-quality journal of Oriental art. Subscriptions available through DPB. $40.00 per year; air-speeded, $44.00.

437. Pal, Pratapaditya. *A Buddhist Paradise: The Murals of Alchi.* Hongkong: Visual Dharma Publications Ltd., 1982. Beautiful full-color plates of a Buddhist monument. DPB $60.00

438. Rice, T. T. *The Ancient Arts of Central Asia.* 1965.

439. Roland, Benjamin. *The Evolution of the Buddha-Image.* New York: Abrams, 1963.

440. *Sacred Art of Tibet,* edited by Tarthang Tulku with introduction by H. V. Guenther. Berkeley: Dharma Publishing, 1975. DPB $7.95

441. Saunders, E. Dale. *Mudrā: A Study of Symbolic Gestures in Japanese Buddhist Sculpture.* Princeton: Princeton University Press, 1960.

442. Schroeder, Ulrich von. *Indo-Tibetan Bronzes.* Hong Kong: Visual Dharma Publications, Inc., 1981.

443. Seckel, Dietrich. *The Art of Buddhism.* New York: Crown, 1964.

444. Sierksma, F. *Tibet's Terrifying Deities.* Rutland, Vt.; Tokyo: Charles E. Tuttle Co., 1966. Text with 43 plates.

445. *The Silk Route and the Diamond Path: Esoteric Buddhist Art on the Trans-Himalayan Trade Routes.* Book catalogue published on the occasion of the exhibition of the same name for UCLA Frederick S. Wright Art Gallery and published through the generosity of the UCLA Art Council. Deborah E. Klimburg-Salter, editor. Los Angeles, 1982. Contains essays, notes, bibliography, and glossary, with many fine plates. DPB $28.00

446. Singh, Madanjeet. *Himalayan Art.* New York: Macmillan, 1971. A small but excellent book with many color plates.

447. Snellgrove, David L., general ed. *The Image of the Buddha.* New York: Kodansha International, 1978. Text beautifully illustrated; includes maps, chronology, and bibliography. DPB $60.00

448. Spink, W. *Ajanta to Ellora.* 1967.

449. *Tibet: A Lost World,* by Valrae Reynolds. New York: American Federation of Arts, 1978. An exhibition catalogue.

450. Tucci, Giuseppe. *The Theory and Practice of the Mandala.* Reprint ed. New York: Samuel Weiser, 1978. A concise study of symbology.

451. Tucci, Giuseppe. *Tibetan Painted Scrolls.* 2 vols. Reprint ed. Kyoto: Rinsen Book Co., 1980. Text on historical, cultural and religious background, with

descriptions and explanation of thankas. Includes sources, documents, and Tibetan texts, together with a separate portfolio of color slides.

452. Watanabe, Y., and Futagawa, Y. *Buddhist Temples in Japan*. Nara, 1962.

453. Weiner, Sheila. *Ajantā: Its Place in Buddhist Art*. Berkeley: University of California Press, 1977.

454. Williams, C. A. S. *Outlines of Chinese Symbolism & Art Motives*. 3rd rev. ed. New York: Dover, 1976. (paperback ed.) First printed in China in 1931; this edition contains many line drawings of symbols found in Confucianism, Taoism, Buddhism, and Lamaism. DPB $6.50

455. Wray, Elizabeth, and Rosefield, Clare. *Ten Lives of the Buddha: Siamese Temple Paintings and Jataka Tales*. New York: Weatherhill, 1972. Beautiful presentation of the Thai religious tradition. DPB $20.00

456. Zimmer, Heinrich. *The Art of Indian Asia*, completed and edited by Joseph Campbell. 2 vols. Princeton: Princeton University Press, 1983. Vol.I, text; vol.II, plates. DPB $32.00/set

457. Zimmer, Heinrich. *Myths and Symbols in Indian Art and Civilization*. Princeton: Princeton University Press, 1953; reprinted 1962. (Bollingen Series 6)

Children's Books

458. *Golden Foot*, illustrated by Rosalyn White. Berkeley: Dharma Publishing, 1976. A moving story of great kindness from the birth stories of the Buddha. Ages 3–10. DPB $4.95

459. *The Hunter and the Quail,* illustrated by Rachel Garbett. Berkeley: Dharma Publishing, 1976. From a Jātaka story on learning to trust one another. Ages 4–10. DPB $4.95

460. *The King and the Mangoes,* illustrated by Sheila Johnson. Berkeley: Dharma Publishing, 1975. From a Jātaka tale about a monkey king who risks his life to lead his tribe to safety. Ages 3-10. DPB $4.95

461. *The Marvelous Companion (Jātakamālā): Life Stories of the Buddha, by Āryaśūra.* Berkeley: Dharma Publishing, 1983. Thirty-four Jātaka tales commmunicate the qualities of the Buddha in his previous lives as a Bodhisattva. Line drawings in the Tibetan style illustrate each story. When read aloud to children, these stories capture the imagination, providing dramatic examples of the importance of unselfish actions. All ages. $25.00

462. *Prince Siddhartha, the Story of Buddha,* written by Jonathan Landaw and illustrated by Janet Brooke. London: Wisdom Publication, 1984. Vivid illustrations, with bright red cover and dust jacket, add to the appeal of this age-old story. For adults as well as children. DPB $15.95

463. *The Proud Peacock and the Mallard,* illustrated by Anne Christman. Berkeley: Dharma Publishing, 1976. A Jātaka tale that warns of false pride and boasting. Ages 4–10. DPB $4.95

464. *The Spade Sage,* adapted from the Jātaka Tales and illustrated by Diane Hall. Berkeley: Dharma Publishing, 1976. A gardener breaks his attachments to the worldly life. Ages 6–12. DPB $4.95

465. *Three Wise Birds,* a Jataka story illustrated by Gary

Nolan. Berkeley: Dharma Publishing, 1976. Ages 6–12. DPB $4.95

466. *Tibetan Fantasies,* by Li Gotami Govinda. Berkeley: Dharma Publishing, 1976. Songs and stories drawn from Tibetan folklore, delightfully illustrated by the author. All ages. DPB $5.95

467. *Tibetan Folk Tales,* translated by Frederich and Audrey Hyde-Chambers and illustrated by Kusho Ralla. Boulder: Shambhala, 1981. Thirty legends and folk tales from the 'Land of Snow', full of humor and love, this collection will appeal to young and old. DPB $7.95

Related Readings and Reference

Related Readings

468. Bly, Robert. *News of the Universe: Poems of the Two-Fold Consciousness.* San Francisco: Sierra Club Books, 1980. DPB $7.95

469. *Buddhism and American Thinkers: The Buddhist American Encounter in Philosophy,* edited by Kenneth K. Inada and Nolan P. Jaakson. Albany: State University of New York, 1984. DPB $9.95

470. Capra, Fritjof. *The Tao of Physics.* 2nd rev. ed. Boulder: Shambhala, 1983. "An exploration of the parallels between modern physics and eastern mysticism." DPB $7.95

471. Deussen, Paul. *The Philosophy of the Upanishads.* Reprint of 1906 ed. New York: Dover Publications, 1966. DPB $5.00

472. Eliade, Mircea. *Yoga, Immortality, and Freedom,* translated by W. R. Trask. 2nd ed. Princeton, 1959. (Bolligen Series 56). Important study for advanced students; includes notes, bibliography, index. DPB $6.95

473. Fields, Rick. *How the Swans Came to the Lake: A Narrative History of Buddhism in America.* Boulder: Shambhala, 1981.

474. Jacobson, Nolan P. *Buddhism and the Contemporary World.* Carbondale: Illinois University Press, 1983.

475. Johnson, Willard. *Riding the Ox Home: A History of Meditation from Shamanism to Science.* London: Rider, 1982. DPB $9.95

476. Martland, Thomas R. *Religion as Art: An Interpretation.* New York: State University of New York, 1983.

477. Nakamura, Hajime. *Ways of Thinking of Eastern Peoples: India, China, Tibet, Japan.* Rev. ed. Honolulu: University of Hawaii Press, 1964.

478. Nilsson, Lennart. *Behold Man: A Photographic Journey of Discovery Inside the Body*. Boston: Little, Brown, & Co., 1974. DPB $19.95

479. Nishitani, Keiji. *Religion and Nothingness.* Berkeley: University of California Press, 1982. Originally entitled *What is Religion?;* also published serially in *Eastern Buddhist,* 1970–1980. DPB $8.95

480. Odin, Steven. *Process Metaphysics and Hua-yen Buddhism: A Critical Study of Cumulative Penetration vs. Interpenetration.* Albany: State University of New York, 1982.

481. Potter, Karl. *Presuppositions of Indian Philosophy.* Englewood Cliffs: Prentice-Hall, 1963.

482. Reischauer, Edwin O., and Fairbank, John K. *East Asia, the Great Tradition.* A History of East Asian Civilization, vol. I. Boston: Houghton Mifflin, 1958–1960. Extensive coverage on China; includes chapters on Korea, Japan, and East Asia on the eve of modernization; with maps, charts, bibliography, and index. 739pp.

483. Reischauer, Edwin O., and Fairbank, John K. *East Asia, the Modern Transformation.* A History of East Asian Civilization, vol. II. London: Allen & Unwin, 1965.

484. *Revelations in Indian Thought in Honor of Professor T. R. V. Murti,* edited by Harold Coward and Krishna Sivaraman. Berkeley: Dharma Publishing, 1977. Includes papers on the philosophy of language, studies in Buddhism, and East/West comparative studies, written by well-known scholars. DPB $25.00

485. Rumi. *Open Secret: Versions of Rumi,* translated by John Moyne and Coleman Barks. Putney, Vt.: Threshold Books, 1984. DPB $7.95

486. *Secret Doctrines of the Tibetan Books of the Dead,* by Detlef I. Lauf. Boulder: Shambhala, 1977. A scholarly work made after study of original texts of both the Buddhist and the Bon religions. Includes psychological commentary, illustrations, and diagrams, with a comparison of Western investigations of death and dying.

487. *The Secret of the Golden Flower: A Chinese Book of Life,* translated by Richard Wilhelm, with foreword and commentary by C. G. Jung. Reprint of 1931 ed. New York: Harcourt Brace Jovanovich, 1962. Contains part of "The Book of Consciousness and Life," a Chinese meditation text. DPB $2.95

488. *Studies in Indian Thought,* the collected papers of Professor T. R. V. Murti, edited by Harold Coward. Delhi: Motilal Banarsidass, 1983.

489. Warder, A. K. *Outline of Indian Philosophy.* Delhi: Motilal Banarsidass, 1971. Based only on original Sanskrit, Pāli, and Prākrit sources; a trustworthy reference. DPB $7.95

490. Zimmer, Heinrich. *The King and the Corpse: Tales of the Soul's Conquest of Evil,* edited by Joseph Campbell. Princeton: Princeton University Press, 1971.

Time, Space, and Knowledge

491. Tarthang Tulku, general editor. *Dimensions of Thought: Current Explorations in Time, Space, and Knowledge,* edited by Ralph Moon and Steven Randall. 2 vols. Berkeley: Dharma Publishing, 1980. Helpful auxillary readings for TSK students.
DPB $8.95/vol.

492. Tarthang Tulku. *Knowledge of Freedom: Time to Change.* Berkeley: Dharma Publishing, 1984. A penetrating inquiry into freedom, lifestyles, mind, and the human response to knowledge; a sound basis for Dharma study, written for the general reader.
DPB $8.50

493. Tarthang Tulku. *Time, Space, and Knowledge: A New Vision of Reality.* Berkeley: Dharma Publishing, 1977. A synthesis of philosophy and personal experience. Includes 35 exercises proven helpful to practitioners; a unique and valuable work which opens the mind to a profound understanding of human potential. With full-color plates.
DPB $9.95

Bibliographies on Buddhism

494. *Bibliographie Bouddhique.* Paris: Librarie Orientaliste Paul Geuthner, 1930–1967. Vols. I–III, 1930–1933, included in *Buddhica,* sér. II, tomes 3, 5, 6.

495. *Bibliographie de Bouddhism, tome I: Éditions de textes.* Bruxelles: Institut Belge des Hautes Études Bouddhiques, 1971. (Série bibliographies 2).

496. *Bibliographie de la Litterature Prajñāpāramitā,* compiled by Pierre Beautrix. Bruxelles: Institut Belge des Hautes Études Bouddhiques, 1971. (Série bibliographies 3).

497. *Bibliography of Asian Studies.* Ann Arbor: Association for Asian Studies, 1946– . Published annually.

498. *Bibliography of Indian Philosophies,* compiled by Karl Potter. Delhi: Motilal Banarsidass, 1970. Supplements in *Journal of Indian Philosophy* 2 (1972):65–112; 4 (1977):295–399.

499. *A Bibliography of Japanese Buddhism,* compiled by Shōjun Bando and others. Tokyo: Cultural Interchange Institute for Buddhists, 1958.

500. "A Bibliography of Tibetan Studies," by Sibadas Chaudhuri. Part I in *Journal of the Asiatic Society of Bengal. Letters* 24,2 (1959): Bibliographic Supplement; parts 2-7 in *Journal of the Asiatic Society of Bengal* 1–4 (1959–1962): Bibliographical Supplements.

501. *Bibliography on Buddhism,* compiled by S. Hanayama. Tokyo: Hokuseido, 1961. Cites entries published up to 1935.

502. *The Blue Annals,* by Gos lo-tsā-ba gZhon-nu dpal, translated by George N. Roerich. Reprint ed. Delhi: Motilal Banarsidass, 1979. Very valuable source for canonical bibliography and Tibetan translation history, with indexes of Sanskrit and Tibetan text titles.

503. *Books on Buddhism, an Annotated Subject Guide,* compiled by Yushin Yoo. Metuchen, N.J.: Scarecrow Press, 1976.

504. *Buddhism: A Select Bibliography,* compiled by Satyaprakash. New Delhi: Indian Documentation Service, 1976.

505. *Buddhism: A Subject Index to Periodical Articles in English, 1928–1971,* compiled by Yushin Yoo. Metuchen, N. J.: Scarecrow Press, 1931.

506. *Buddhism in India, Ceylon, China, and Japan: A Reader's Guide,* by Clarence H. Hamilton. Chicago: University of Chicago Press, 1931.

507. *Buddhist Text Information.* Stony Brook, New York: Center for the Advanced Study of World Religions. 1– 1974– . A quarterly publication with cumulative indexes.

508. *Der buddhistische Kanon. Eine Bibliographie,* compiled by Günter Grönbold. Wiesbaden: Harrassowitz, 1984.

509. "A Contribution to the Bibliography of Tibet," compiled by J. van Manen. *Journal of the Asiatic Society of Bengal,* n.s. 18 (1925):445–525.

510. *Catalogue of the Library of Tibetan Works and Archives Reference Department,* compiled by G. Dekhang. Dharamsala: Library of Tibetan Works & Archives, 1981.

511. *Cumulative Bibliography of Asian Studies, 1941–* sponsored by the Association for Asian Studies. Boston: G. K. Hall.

512. *Deutsche Bibliographie des Buddhismus,* compiled by Hans Ludwig Held. Hildesheim: N. Y. G. Olms, 1973. A guide to German language publications.

513. *Guide to Buddhist Religion,* by Frank E. Reynolds, John Holt, and John Strong. Boston: G. K. Hall, 1981.

514. *Guide to the Literature of Khotan,* by R. E. Em-

merick. Tokyo: The Reiyukai Library, 1979. A bibliographical survey of Khotanese Buddhist texts.

515. *Indian Buddhism,* by A. K. Warder. 2nd rev.ed. Delhi: Motilal Banarsidass, 1980. Extensive bibliography, pp. 523–569. DPB $25.00

516. *Indian Buddhism: A Survey with Bibliographical Notes,* by Hajime Nakamura. Hirataka (Japan): Kansai University of Foreign Studies, 1980. Particularly useful for works by Japanese scholars.

517. "Non-Canonical Pali Literature," by Bimala Churn Law. *Annals of the Bhandarkar Oriental Research Institute, Poona* 13, 2 (1932):97–143.

518. *The Nyingma Edition of the sDe-dge bKa'-'gyur/bsTan-'gyur. Research Catalogue and Bibliography.* Tarthang Tulku, director. 8 vols. Berkeley: Dharma Publishing, 1982. Vols. 1–7: bibliographies of published editions and translations of canonical texts, listed text by text; vol. 8: listings of Sanskrit manuscripts, a bibliography of Pāli texts, and a select bibliography of works useful to canonical studies. With indexes of modern editors and authors.

519. *Pāli Buddhist Texts Explained to the Beginner,* by R. E. A. Johansson. Rev. ed. London: Curzon Press, 1977. (Scandinavian Institute of Asian Studies. Monograph Series 14)

520. "Pāli Literature," by Wilhelm Geiger, chapter 1 of *Pāli Literature and Language.* Calcutta: University of Calcutta, 1943. pp. 1–59.

521. *Pāli Literature,* including the canonical literature in Prakrit and Sanskrit of all the Hīnayāna schools

of Buddhism, by K. R. Norman. Wiesbaden: Harrassowitz, 1982.

522. *Prague Collection of Tibetan Prints from sDe-dge,* by J. Kolmas. 2 vols. Wiesbaden: Harrassowitz, 1971. (Asiatische Forschungen 36). Facsimile reproductions of 5,615 book titles printed at the dGon-chen and dPal-sprung monasteries in Eastern Tibet.

523. *The Prajñāpāramitā Literature,* by Edward Conze. 2nd rev. ed. Tokyo: The Reiyukai Library, 1978. (Bibliographia Philologica Buddhica. Series Maior 1).

524. "Recent Buddhist Studies in Europe and America: 1973–1983," by J. W. de Jong. *Eastern Buddhist* 17,1 (1984):79–107. A useful source for current information on scholarly activities and translations.

525. *Sarvāstivāda Literature,* by A. C. Banerjee. Reprint of 1957 ed. Calcutta: World Press Ltd., 1979. Analyzes Vinaya and Abhidharma texts of the northern Buddhist tradition.

526. *A Survey of Buddhist Sogdian Studies,* by David A. Utz. Tokyo: The Reiyukai Library, 1980.

527. *A Systematic Survey of Buddhist Sanskrit Literature. Vinaya Texte,* compiled by Akira Yuyama. Wiesbaden: Franz Steiner Verlag, 1979. A concise and complete listing of Vinaya texts and translations relating to the northern tradition.

528. *A Union List of Printed Indic Texts and Translations in American Libraries,* by Murray B. Emeneau. New Haven: American Oriental Society, 1935; reprint ed. New York: Kraus, 1968. (American Oriental Series 7). Includes a section on Buddhist texts, nos. 3396a-3913.

Dictionaries of Buddhism

529. *Abingdon Dictionary of Living Religions.* Keith Krim, general ed. Nashville: Abingdon Press, 1981.

530. *A Buddhist Dictionary,* by Nyanatiloka Mahathera. 4th ed. Kandy: Buddhist Publication Society, 1982.

531. *A Dictionary of Buddhism: Indian & South-East Asia,* by Trevor O. Ling. New Delhi: K. P. Bagchi, 1981. (Indological Series 2). Distributed by Humanities Press, Atlantic Highlands, N. J.

532. *A Dictionary of Chinese Buddhist Terms,* compiled by W. E. Soothill and L. Hodous. Reprint ed. Delhi: Motilal Banarsidass, 1977. Includes Sanskrit and English equivalents, and Sanskrit-Pāli index.

533. *Encyclopedia of Buddhism,* edited by G. P. Malalasekera. Sri Lanka: Government of Sri Lanka, 1963– . 12 volumes available at present (A–Bu).

534. *Handbook of Chinese Buddhism,* compiled by E. Eitel. Reprint ed. San Francisco: Chinese Materials Center, 1976. A Sanskrit/Chinese dictionary with vocabularies of Buddhist terms.

535. *Iconographical Dictionary of the Indian Religions: Hinduism, Buddhism, Jainism,* by Gösta Liebert. Leiden: Brill, 1976.

Glossaries of Buddhist Terms; Translation Aids

536. *An Index to the Lankāvatāra Sūtra,* by D. T. Suzuki. 2nd rev. ed. Kyoto: Sanskrit Buddhist Texts Publication Society, 1934. Chinese/Sanskrit, Tibetan/Sanskrit indexes.

537. *Index to the Larger Sukhāvatīvyūha Sūtra: A Tibetan Glossary with Sanskrit and Chinese Equivalents,* by Hisao Inagaki. Kyoto: Nagata Bunshodo, 1978.

538. *Mahāvyutpatti,* prepared by R. Sakaki. 2 vols. Tokyo: Suzuki Research Foundation, 1916. Sanskrit, Tibetan, Japanese.

539. *Materials for a Dictionary of the Prajñāpāramitā Literature,* by Edward Conze. Tokyo: Suzuki Research Foundation, 1973. Sanskrit, Tibetan, English.

540. *Prajñā: Lexicon/Dictionary Portions of the Sanskrit-Tibetan Thesaurus-cum Grammar.* Gangtok, Sikkim: Namgyal Institute of Tibetology, 1961. Sanskrit/Tibetan equivalents of Buddhist terms.

Pāli Dictionaries and Grammars

541. *A Critical Pāli Dictionary,* begun by V. Trenckner, revised, continued, and edited by Dines Andersen & Helmer Smith. Copenhagen: The Royal Danish Academy, 1924-1948. Reprint edition in progress; vols. 1-2 published to date.

542. *Dictionary of Pāli Proper Names,* compiled by G. P. Malalasekera. 2 vols. Reprint ed. London: Pali Text Society, 1974.

543. *Introduction to Pāli,* by A. K. Warder. Reprint of 1963 ed. London: Pali Text Society, 1974.

544. *Pāli-English Dictionary,* edited by T. W. Rhys-Davids and William Stede. Reprint ed. London: Pāli Text Society, 1979.

Sanskrit Dictionaries and Grammars

545. *Buddhist Hybrid Sanskrit Grammar and Dictionary*, by Franklin Edgerton. 2 vols. Reprint ed. Delhi: Motilal Banarsidass, 1972.

546. Burrow, T. *The Sanskrit Language*. 3rd ed. London: Faber & Faber, 1977. An excellent resource for the history, phonology, and grammar of Sanskrit.

547. *A Sanskrit-English Dictionary*, by M. Monier-Williams. Reprint ed. Oxford: Clarendon Press, 1970. An authoritative work for Sanskrit studies.

548. Whitney, William Dwight. *Sanskrit Grammar*, including both the classical language and the older dialects of Veda and Brahmana. 13th ed. Cambridge, Mass.: Harvard University Press, 1973.

Tibetan Dictionaries and Grammars

549. *Dhammapada*. Tibetan text, English translation, vocabulary, glossary of basic technical Buddhist terms, and explanation of Tibetan grammar. Berkeley: Dharma Publishing. Forthcoming 1985. Prepared for the beginning student of Tibetan.

The Divine Tree: A Tibetan Mnemonic Grammar Poem, translated by Noble Ross Reat. Dharamsala: Library of Tibetan Works & Archives, 1982.

551. *A Tibetan-English Dictionary with Sanskrit Synonyms*, by Sarat Chandra Das. Concise edition. Kyoto: Rinsen Book Co., 1983. First published 1902. Contains many Sanskrit equivalents of Tibetan terms; very useful for students of Tibetan.

DPB $40.00

552. *A Tibetan-English Dictionary with English-Tibetan Vocabulary,* by H. A. Jäschke. Reprint ed. Delhi: Motilal Banarsidass, 1975. First published 1881. Very useful for students of Tibetan. DPB $20.00

553. *Tibetan-Russian-English Dictionary with Sanskrit Parallels,* by Y. N. Roerich. 11 vols. Moscow: USSR Academy of Sciences, Institute of Oriental Studies, 1983.

554. *Tibetan-Sanskrit Dictionary,* by Lokesh Chandra. 2 vols. Reprint ed. Kyoto: Rinsen Book Co., 1976.

Catalogues of the Buddhist Canons

555. *An Analysis of the Pāli Canon,* by Russell Webb. Kandy: Buddhist Publications Society, 1975. (The Wheel Publications 217–220). Includes bibliographies.

556. *A Catalogue of the Chinese Translation of the Buddhist Tripiṭaka,* compiled by Bunyiu Nanjio. Reprint of 1883 ed. New Delhi: International Academy of Indian Culture, 1980. Catalogues the Ming edition of the Chinese Canon.

557. *A Catalogue of the Tohoku University Collection of Tibetan Works on Buddhism,* compiled by Y. Kanakura, R. Yamada, T. Tada, and K. Hanada. Sendai, 1953.

558. *A Catalogue of the Urga Kanjur in the Prof. Raghuvira Collection at the International Academy of Indian Culture,* by Geza Bethlenfalvy. New Delhi, 1980 (Śatapiṭaka Series, Indo-Asian Literatures, 246) Catalogues a rare edition of the Tibetan bKa'-'gyur carved in Ulan Bator, Mongolia.

559. *Comparative Catalogue of Chinese Āgamas and Pāli Nikāyas,* by Chizen Akanuma. Nagoya: Hajinkaku Shobō, 1929. An important reference for students interested in comparing the Pāli and Chinese traditions.

560. *Guide to the Nyingma Edition of the sDe-dge bKa'-'gyur/bsTan-'gyur,* edited by Tarthang Tulku. 2 vols. Berkeley: Dharma Publishing, 1983.

561. *The Korean Buddhist Canon: A Descriptive Catalogue,* prepared by Lewis Lancaster. Berkeley: University of California Press, 1980. A catalogue of the Koryō edition of the Chinese Canon.

562. *The Nyingma Edition of the sDe-dge bKa'-'gyur/bsTan-'gyur,* edited by Tarthang Tulku. 120 vols., with an 8 vol. Catalogue/Bibliography. Berkeley: Dharma Publishing, 1981. Catalogue/Bibliography published in 1982.

563. *Tables du Taishō Issaikyō,* compiled by Sylvain Lévi and Junjirō Takakusu. Hōbōgirin, Fascicule Annexe. Tokyo: Maison Franco-Japonaise, 1931. Index to the Taishō edition of the Chinese Canon.

564. "The Tibetan Tripiṭaka," by Kenneth Ch'en, in *Harvard Journal of Asian Studies* 9 (1945–1947):53–62. Not a catalogue, but a useful overview of the editions of the Tibetan Canon.

565. "The Written Tradition." *Crystal Mirror VII,* edited by Tarthang Tulku. Berkeley: Dharma Publishing, 1984. pp. 203–251. Overview of the oral transmission, dissemination of manuscripts and their recovery during the past centuries, and helpful details of translations of texts into Asian languages. Includes

information on the compilation of the Chinese, Pāli, Tibetan, Mongolian, Hsi-hsia, and Manchu Canons with their printing and publication histories.

Journals

The following list of journals contain many articles on Buddhism and related information. They are available at most major college and university libraries.

566. *Bulletin de l'École Française d'Extrême-Orient.*
567. *Bulletin of the London School of Oriental and African Studies.*
568. *Eastern Buddhist.*
569. *Harvard Journal of Asiatic Studies.*
570. *History of Religions.*
571. *Indo-Iranian Journal.*
572. *Journal of Buddhist Philosophy.*
573. *Journal of Indian Philosophy.*
574. *Journal of the International Association of Buddhist Studies.*
575. *The Middle Way.*
576. *Philosophy East and West.*

Dharma Publishing Bookstore

Dharma Publishing Bookstore, located at the Nyingma Institute, serves faculty and students with texts and reference materials for classroom use. The Bookstore is open to the general public, and invites people interested in Dharma books to visit and investigate its collection. In addition to a complete line of Dharma Publishing books, posters, and Dharmart Designs greeting cards, the Bookstore stocks books on Buddhism and related subjects from other publishers in India, Japan, Europe, and America.

Books that can be supplied by the Bookstore are indicated with the intials DPB together with price information. The Bookstore offers worldwide mail-order service, and welcomes special orders. Although some books listed in this bibliography are out of print, many are available in libraries or from used book dealers in the United States, Canada, or Europe.

Because of consistent demand, a number of books on Buddhism have lately been reprinted; while prices are not always listed here, it is possible that the books are now available and could be supplied upon request. The staff of the Bookstore has current information about the status of most of the books mentioned in this bibliography, and invites inquiries from interested readers.

Ordering Information

Please make check or money order payable to Dharma Publishing Bookstore. All orders must be prepaid. California customers please add 6% sales tax; in Bart counties, 6½%.

Add shipping and handling costs to price of book(s) as follows:

Bookpost: Allow 3–5 weeks for delivery. Cost: $1.50 for first book plus $0.75 for each additional book. Shipping for each 2 volume cloth set, $3.50.

UPS: Allow 1–2 weeks for delivery. UPS accepts street addresses only. Cost: $2.50 for first book plus $1.00 for each additional book. Shipping for each 2 volume cloth set, $4.75.

Book Surface Mail (for orders outside the U.S.): Allow 6–8 weeks for delivery. Cost: $2.00 for first book plus $0.75 for each additional book. Shipping for each 2 volume cloth set, $5.00.

The Bookstore cannot accept responsibility for books lost or damaged in transit. If desired, the Bookstore can ship books insured; insurance costs will be quoted upon request. Due to fluctuating publisher's prices and values of foreign currency, prices may be subject to change without notice.

Address all orders and inquiries to:

Dharma Publishing Bookstore
1815 Highland Place Berkeley, CA 94709

(415) 843-6812

Dharma Publishing Books

Nyingma Translation Series

Voice of the Buddha (Lalitavistara Sūtra)
The Marvelous Companion (Jātakamālā)
Life and Liberation of Padmasambhava
Kindly Bent to Ease Us
Mother of Knowledge
Buddha's Lions
Calm and Clear
Elegant Sayings
Golden Zephyr
Legend of the Great Stupa
Mind in Buddhist Psychology
Dhammapada

Nyingma Psychology Series

Reflections of Mind
Gesture of Balance
Openness Mind
Kum Nye Relaxation
Skillful Means
Hidden Mind of Freedom
Knowledge of Freedom: Time to Change

Time, Space, and Knowledge

Time, Space, and Knowledge
Dimensions of Thought

Children's Books

The Spade Sage
Three Wise Birds
The King and the Mangoes
Golden Foot
The Hunter and the Quail
The Proud Peacock and the Mallard
Tibetan Fantasies

Additional Publications

Sacred Art of Tibet
Copper Mountain: The Odiyan Mandala
Annals of the Nyingma Lineage in America
Psychocosmic Symbolism of the Buddhist Stupa
Buddhist Thought and Asian Civilization
Tibetan Buddhism in Western Perspective
Revelations in Indian Thought
Tibet in Pictures
Zen Philosophy, Zen Practice
Crystal Mirror, vols. 1-7
Gesar, Magazine of Buddhism in the West

Dharma Publishing

2425 Hillside Avenue, Berkeley, CA 94704 U.S.A.